Praise for *Heaven on Earth*

"This book brings such serenity. In a masterful gesture, Stephanie Dowrick has collected prayers from these days back to earliest centuries. All the prayers, including some by the author herself, are arranged in a mosaic pattern that leads us towards the oneness we all long for. I urge you to open this book and read one or two prayers whenever you feel the need to see your shrink . . . or are seeking instant peace."
— **Hanan al-Shaykh**, author of *The Locust and the Bird*

"Each person who picks up *Heaven on Earth* will discover many wonderful choices that she has brought together in one easy-to-use book for connecting with the One and with your own inner strength during the ups and downs of daily life. In addition, she supports and encourages each of our unique and different ways of going to that healing inner space of holiness that is beyond words. Her openness and non-judgmentalness are extra benefits of this book and very timely."
— **Leonard Felder**, PhD, author of *Here I Am: Using Jewish Spiritual Wisdom to Become More Present, Centered, and Available for Life*

"Just as prayer moves us, this book moves me. By showing us how to find the presence of God, Dowrick restores our confidence in humanity. This is a profound and immensely helpful contribution, at a time when we need it the most—not one wasted page."
— **Jeff Golliher**, Episcopal priest and author of *A Deeper Faith* and *Moving Through Fear*

"Stephanie Dowrick has written and compiled a wonderful interfaith resource and companion for anyone seeking to deepen their inner life. *Heaven on Earth* is a feast for the spirit."
— **Rev. Diane Berke**, founder and spiritual director, One Spirit Interfaith Seminary

"Stephanie Dowrick's sensitivity as a teacher and writer provides the reader with a unique collection that reminds us that we find divinity most profoundly in *relationship*. In speaking the words of these prayers the reader will not only find solace, but also meaningful relationship with a world that is both subjective and sacred. *Heaven on Earth* is not so much a book for us to merely read and put on the shelf as it is one to carry with us in hand and heart on our journeys."
— **Theodore Richards**, author of *Cosmosophia* and *Creatively Maladjusted: The Wisdom Education Movement Manifesto*

"Truthfully, Stephanie, all your prayers are divine. They speak to me as if I had made them up. They speak the words that are from my soul too. You have a great gift to write about the universality of being human and enable us who read your work to feel, in some very meaningful way, 'You wrote this just for me.'"
— **Sharon Snir**, psychotherapist and author of *The Little Book of Everyday Miracles*

"Wrap yourself in beautiful words and spiritual connection in times of fear, grief or simply reflection. These writings will transport you back to your core and wipe the slate clean. If you want the gift of prayer, give yourself the gift of this book."
— **Laura Berman Fortgang**, author of *The Little Book on Meaning*

"Stephanie Dowrick offers us her wise insight into the transformative qualities of prayer, as well as an interfaith anthology that will become a precious resource to so many. Available to all, prayer can be great equalizing force for good, an instrument of personal and societal healing, a repair of what has been broken. Including her own prayers with those of many spiritual traditions, this book is an act of love by a writer devoted to the sacred."
— **Joyce Kornblatt**, meditation and writing teacher and author of *The Reason for Wings*

continued . . .

"Whether or not you are in the habit of praying, whether or not you believe in a traditional God, this mosaic of prayers gathered from around the world will delight and inspire."

—**Susan Katz Miller**, author of *Being Both: Embracing Two Religions in One Interfaith Family*

"Stephanie Dowrick gives prayer back to the reader like a precious gift that was somehow forgotten or mislaid. I carry a different feeling about prayer around with me since reading these beautiful pages. Prayer helps set my compass towards the highest. A generous and joyful book.".

—**Dr. Juliet Batten**, author of *A Cup of Sunlight* and *Spirited Ageing*

"A fabulous read, a real feast! Whatever stage you are at in your prayer life, you will discover how instinctive prayer is and how praying can bring out your true self in times of darkness and joy."

—**Rosalind Bradley**, author of *A World of Prayer*

"Gently leading us into a deeply felt experience of prayer, you can tell instantly that prayer is not something Stephanie Dowrick does—it is central to who she is. 'Prayer moves us,' she says, and I also found myself equally moved by her heartfelt book on prayer."

—**August Gold**, coauthor of *Multiply Your Blessings* and *The Prayer Chest*

"Stephanie Dowrick is emphatic that the Divine is accessible to all and not a dogmatic prerogative of the few. Stephanie's own prayers reveal how she embraces and feels embraced by God. Whilst contemplating her prayers one feels that Divine Hug. Her prayers give us the confidence and the compass on how to open our own hearts in trust and friendship to the Sacred."

—**Anthony Strano**, BK meditation teacher and author of *Seeking Silence*

"Since I was a teenager, Stephanie Dowrick's work has been absolutely central to my understanding of curiosity, spirit, faith and the possibility of happiness. Her words speak about faith and longing and hope in ways that people like me can be heartened by. The wisdom in her pages has comforted me in dark times and brought me insights that I fear I may otherwise have missed. With deep intelligence and enormous heart, Stephanie has written and interpreted these prayers, creating a well-loved companion for anyone seeking beauty, comfort and insight." —**Clare Bowditch**, musician

"Stephanie Dowrick sees prayer as the constant tuning of heart and mind to the bounty of Kabir's 'single kind of love' that is directly recognized in all streams of contemplative practice, however differently they may name it. Her volume of prompts towards that open state is bounty in its own right."

—**Dr. Susan Murphy**, Zen roshi and author of *Minding the Earth, Mending the World*

"These stunning prayers and poems embody the Timeless, the Traditional, and the Beyond. Stephanie Dowrick emerges as a mystical poet with a radiance of her own in the company of those whose words she has chosen."

—**Dr. Marj Britt**, vice president of the Academic Governance Council, board of Unity Institute and Seminary

"In this marvelous collection, Dr. Stephanie Dowrick offers what so many of us desire: an authentic invitation into the mystery of prayer. This is a book to cherish. But more than this, it is one to *use* as a pathway into greater awareness, deeper connection, and a more profound sense of gratitude for the gift of life. What could be more welcome in times like these, when a trustworthy guide to the spiritual life like this one is so urgently needed?"

—**Dr. Mark S. Burrows**, professor of theology and spirituality and author of a new translation of Rainer Maria Rilke's *Prayers of a Young Poet*

HEAVEN

on

EARTH

HEAVEN

on

EARTH

Timeless Prayers of Wisdom and Love

STEPHANIE DOWRICK

JEREMY P. TARCHER/PENGUIN

a member of Penguin Group (USA)

New York

JEREMY P. TARCHER/PENGUIN
Published by the Penguin Group
Penguin Group (USA) LLC, 375 Hudson Street,
New York, New York 10014, USA

USA · Canada · UK · Ireland · Australia
New Zealand · India · South Africa · China

penguin.com
A Penguin Random House Company

Most Tarcher/Penguin books are available at special quantity discounts for bulk
purchase for sales promotions, premiums, fund-raising, and educational needs.
Special books or book excerpts also can be created to fit specific needs.
For details, write: Special.Markets@us.penguingroup.com.

Library of Congress Cataloging-in-Publication Data

Dowrick, Stephanie.
Heaven on earth : timeless prayers of wisdom and love / Stephanie Dowrick.
p.   cm.
Includes index.
ISBN 978-0-399-16448-4
1. Prayers.   I. Title.
BL560.D69   2013   2013017167
204'.33—dc23

Printed in the United States of America
1 3 5 7 9 10 8 6 4 2

BOOK DESIGN BY AMANDA DEWEY

Prayer is a longing of the soul. . . .
and an instrument of action.

—*Mahatma Gandhi*

The function of prayer is not to influence God,
but rather to change the nature
of the one who prays.

—*Søren Kierkegaard*

Prayer cannot bring water to parched fields,
mend a broken bridge, or rebuild a broken city,
but prayer can water an arid soul,
mend a broken heart,
and rebuild a weakened will.

—*Rabbi Abraham Joshua Heschel*

Every fear falls away as we enter into Thee
and Thy glory of love,
and as we bask in the sunshine of love,
Thy love,
Thy never-failing love!

—*Charles and Cora Fillmore*

Contents

For my dear friends Hilary Star and Judith Ackroyd:

Peace be with you and in our world.

Prayer Is Itself
an "Answer"

Sitting in my quiet study, books piled on my workbench, first spring daffodils in a jug, our aged gray cat on a stool next to mine, sounds from the street reaching me in familiar ways, my uppermost thought is what a privilege it has been to collect these prayers of wisdom and love. It's been a privilege and a joy to write some of them, adapt others, to pray all of them—and share them.

Writing must always be a work of love and, as I have discovered, that is particularly true when the writing is about prayer and is offering prayers that could bring you greater happiness, consolation, security, insight and hope.

The most profound encouragement in my own life comes from prayer. So does the greatest solace. And the good news is that no one needs to become a prayer expert to discover this. In fact, the fifteenth-century poet Kabir, one of history's most exuberant spiritual teachers, urges: "Put your cleverness aside. Learning alone will not unite you with the Divine. Love is something far greater. Those who seek it, find it."

In other words, *dive in*. Experiment! Find out for yourself. Learn through the variety of your own experiences. However tentative it may be, hear the call of prayer and touch life more deeply, sensually and gratefully.

What's also poignant and remarkable is just how faithfully prayer rewards us. That's something I have discovered and re-discovered not in the easiest but in the hardest and most barren times. Praying, I am no longer alone. Praying, I have something more than my everyday frailties to call on. Praying, I become myself and exceed myself. Praying, my whole self is present: mind, body, heart, spirit and soul. Praying, however incoherently in times of grief and desolation, healing seems possible.

There were years in my younger adult life when I scarcely prayed at all, when the demands of the outer world seemed impossibly urgent and prayer seemed distanced from me and I from it. Yet even in those most distracted times, I continued to feel drawn to prayer. I also remained entranced by stories of prayer's power.

When I did return to prayer, it was mostly wordless: a reaching out that needed to be felt rather than formulated. I've no doubt that this was in part because I needed to recover from years and layers of "prayer words" that hadn't worked for me—that had diminished my sense of myself and distanced me from the sacred rather than making it more real. In that potent silence, I discovered prayer's subtle, powerful rewards. I learned how essential listening is to a life of prayer. *"Be still, and know that I am God."* And I learned how transformative it is when words of loving encouragement take us into the silence, and out of it again.

Words do matter, though. They create our perceptions and our truths. In fact, it's through the stories we tell ourselves that we interpret and "see" the world. Words have the power to harm—and to heal. And it's words that carry the prayers in this collection directly to your mind and heart.

Praying in twenty-first-century life, we are free to use words and to choose the words that will serve us best. The words in the prayers that I have included in this collection will unfailingly reflect back to you the very best of who you are. And that matters. Until we recognize our power for connectedness, joy, compassion, kindness, hope and forgiveness, we risk assuming that those are qualities for special people, but not for us.

This freedom to choose our words and to choose how we will pray is relatively new and very precious. This is because, truly, we do not simply pray: we are also "prayed" by what we choose to have on our lips or in our thoughts and hearts.

Giving ourselves the gift of reading or remembering a prayer, we are tuning our minds no less effectively than a string musician tunes her instrument before playing it. Whatever the prayer, whatever the words, praying is ultimately an act of hope. It is also an act of connection and of trust. In its quiet, exquisite way, prayer deepens our knowledge of who we are and what life is for.

Prayer takes us beyond ordinary thinking. It *moves* us. It brings us home to the intimacy of the heart, even as it's connecting us to the dimensions we call infinite. Its sweep is vast, and vastly subtle. A life secured by prayer brings hope, possibility and comfort. It brings vital insight. It makes the world new each day.

Prayer brings beauty alive, too. And teaches us what beauty truly is. True prayer opens our eyes as well as our hearts. It softens as well as strengthens us. Some of the most tender, beautiful and affecting prayers in this collection are prayers to say in time of need when life seems anything but beautiful. And that's not by chance. To find beauty and to renew hope in a time of raw vulnerability can literally be lifesaving.

Who hasn't learned most about prayer by needing prayer: needing it when all the usual strategies seem agonizingly empty? We even speak of "falling on our knees" in such moments. There's courage in that as well as humility. Falling on our knees, literally or figuratively, or simply turning inward, we discover a resource that has guided, fulfilled and inspired our human family since time immemorial.

We may also discover within ourselves the depth of our own longing for all that prayer can bring. And for what prayer does bring, for prayer itself *is* relationship, connecting mind and heart and spirit through wisdom and love, and re-making us whole.

I am not alone in discovering this, yet it is a discovery that no one else can make for us. Almost twenty years ago, when my familiar world was falling apart in more ways than one, and my precious, beloved children were still very young, completely dependent, and I feared that I could die and leave them, as my own mother had when I was only eight and my sister eleven, I was compelled to pray. I had had years of meditation and what had passed for a reasonably committed prayer life. But now I prayed fiercely and desperately.

This isn't new. Human fear and anguish are not new. Nor is our response to them. We hear such frantic need reflected in the Psalms (*"Out of the depths I cry to you, O Lord. Lord, hear my voice"*). Many of us have heard similar pleas arising spontaneously in our mouths and hearts. And in that harsh year of illness and loss of trust, I too had to discover a quite new depth of prayer because nothing else would work or do.

I was by then a trained psychotherapist, an experienced writer on psychological and spiritual matters, and someone with family and friends who loved and love me. For all that, I felt empty and desperate. In fact, I sometimes felt that my years of professional training and personal therapy simply mocked the new reality of my life. "Answers" and especially explanations felt arid. I needed more. I needed the depth, and that peculiar mixture of spaciousness and closeness, that only prayer could give me.

Many years later, and after working with countless people in diverse retreat and ministry situations, I am grateful for what I learned from that time, while also being honest enough to freely admit that I wish I could have learned it any other way. I am not *grateful* for the harsher experiences of my life. I am, though, certainly thankful that somehow I was pushed from within to accept what the experience of prayer could give me.

Prayer is, of course, about more than our cries of desperate need. It is and can soon become a way of living. It's about more than praise, too, even while it includes and extends praise, celebration, gratitude, delight and even humor. But whatever its mood or tenor, from whatever place we begin—and however often we begin again—prayer is most reliably about *receiving*. "Your Love, O God," wrote monk and writer Thomas Merton before his untimely death in 1968, "speaks to my life as to an intimate in the midst of a crowd of strangers."

In prayer, that most precious intimacy is possible. One of the most exquisite promises attributed to Jesus assures us: "*Come to me, all you who struggle and are burdened. Come to me and I will give you rest.*"

There is no sense here of "Stand up straight. Learn your lines. Put on your Sabbath best and then I will see whether I have time for you." No, the welcome to return to love is unconditional, and unconditionally consoling.

Letting your eyes close or allowing them to rest on inspirational words, pausing between the hectic moments of everyday existence, turning your thoughts inward and, simultaneously, beyond yourself: you pray. And you are prayed.

It delights me that so much can emerge from what seems to be so little. Yet I am also aware that prayer takes place inside that most private of all places: your own mind. This is true even when you share words and pray communally—which may make it difficult for some of you to know quite where you are on the prayer continuum. You might have lost your desire to pray, or you might be dealing with old layers of disappointment around prayer. You might wonder whether the time you make for prayer is time wasted. *Who's listening?* And if "anyone" *is* listening, who's caring?

Or perhaps you are reasonably sure that prayer itself is worthwhile but much less sure if your own prayers and praying are "worthy." You might wonder if other people pray more fervently or faithfully than you do, or if they get rewards from prayer that are more tangible and more immediate.

Those concerns are totally understandable. But they lead you away from prayer, rather than toward it. Prayer is not like personal training for the spirit! Your usual equations of effort and reward are barely relevant. And what a relief that is.

Commitment is something different. Commitment benefits anyone willing to pray and to reflect or meditate prayerfully. Yet even when that commitment is highly tentative, as it was for me for many years, prayer waits patiently. Prayer is not a duty. It's not something you must do to impress God or win rewards. Prayer is itself a limitless reward.

Given the slightest chance, prayer pours itself into us. The words are like a vehicle for the energy that is prayer. Sufi poet Rumi is famous for saying that there is no quicker way to God than praying. He also pointed out that "Praying is only the external form. The soul of the prayer is infinite. . . ."

It's with amazement sometimes and gratitude, too, that I have discovered how prayer opens the way for us. It is literally the light in the darkness and does not ever rebuke us. Effort, trying, duty or excellence . . . these are not useful ways to think about prayer: that small, often muted act founded on hope, love, wonder, gratitude, insight, discovery and the human need for connection and profound consolation.

By opening to prayers that are both loving and affirming, your vision of life—and your understanding of your own life's meaning— will take a turn for the better. I am quite sure of that. Using prayers of love as your foundation for life, prayer will refine your thinking and put "thinking" in its place.

When it comes to prayer and praying, *surrender* seems a better word than *effort*. One of the most famous prayers of all expresses this: "*Not my will, but Thine be done.*" But by *surrender* I also mean a willingness to give up some of your old ideas about prayer in order to discover what prayer itself will teach you, little bit by precious little bit.

A life of prayer often begins with that longing for help or answers that I so urgently needed. Yet one of the loveliest discoveries that I have made from my own sometimes irreverent but increasingly committed lifetime of prayer is that *prayer is itself an answer*. In all its dimensions, it gathers us in when we feel scattered. It heals hurts (though sometimes in unexpected ways). It is steadying. And it's certainly the fastest way I know to take us home to the heart.

It is intrinsically restorative to pray. It anchors us. It brings life back when our faith in life is diminished. It settles us. It opens our hearts.

It is also wonderfully natural to pray. In fact, it would seem that the impulse to pray crosses religions, cultures and time itself. In fear, people cry out, "God help me!" In relief, they say, "Thank God!" In joy or surprise, they say, "My God!" Theists, atheists: we all do it.

Praying brings depth to the most ordinary events. Some of the most tender prayers you will find in these pages are those that you can say first thing in the morning or last thing at night with your loved ones of any age, or that you can share with children or grandchildren as you gather to enjoy a meal or to express gratitude for each day.

With the pause that prayer brings, we see how the everyday moments of a life do *matter*. Public and private rituals of prayer join us to one another, and join us over the centuries to untold generations of our human family. And not just to the people most like us, either. Prayer also connects us, implicitly as well as explicitly, with people who we may have assumed to be quite unlike "us." *"O Lord,"* prayed the seventeenth-century English bishop Thomas Ken, *"we ask that you will make the door of this church, and of our lives, wide enough to receive all who need human love and fellowship, and the care of Divine love . . . Make this a gateway to our knowledge of eternity. May we bring heaven to earth."*

Praying may also free us from the need to ask, "Why me?" Praying, we soften or lose our fear of meaninglessness or abandonment. *"Even darkness is not dark to you, O Lord. To you the darkest night is bright as the day,"* we hear in Psalm 139. And from the even older Bhagavad Gita come these sublime lines: *"I am always with all beings; I abandon no one. However great your sorrows, you are never separated from me."* Praying is a

sublime way to restore hope . . . not necessarily in a particular outcome, but in life itself and our place within it.

But what if you want or need to pray yet are uncertain about the
idea of a personal relationship with God, or even about the idea of
God or a Higher Power?

For you, also, prayer is meaningful, not least as a deepening experience of the sacred within life. Whatever our beliefs, the act of prayer
is an avowal that we can and sometimes must extend hope beyond our
daily resources. It is an affirmation of the intimacy as well as the mystery of spirituality, a sacred view of life that does not always depend
on an intimacy with God. In fact, the commitment and fervor with
which many Buddhists pray offers countless examples of this.

The God to whom I pray—and the God you will meet here—is
the Divine Source, the universal Beloved celebrated in the mystical
and wisdom traditions. This is a "relationship God": beyond human
characterizing but not beyond human experiencing; a God embracing, wholly loving, and ceaselessly transforming how we understand
who and what we are and are capable of being. This is a you-God
connection caught by visionary poet Rainer Maria Rilke (in Mark
Burrows's powerful English translation) when he suggests: *"You must
know that God blows through you/ from the beginning."*

Yet such a connection—or even the yearning for it—is not essential for an active, sustaining prayer life. We have only to look around
our own communities to witness how diversely people explore and
enter the sacred. "To me, mindfulness is very much like the Holy
Spirit," Zen monk and peacemaker Thich Nhat Hanh has written.
"Both are agents of healing."

Prayer is itself a most powerful "agent of healing." It is a way of
touching life and being touched by it; of being mindful of what is
needed, and open to what can be received. It's a meeting point

between the temporal and eternal that is sacramental in its potency. Prayer has certainly changed the way I personally experience and seek God. It has taken obligation totally out of the picture. (I don't pray or seek to discover meaning or goodness because I *should*, or because I think otherwise God will abandon or punish me. I pray because I can.) And still prayer does more than that.

Prayer can change the way we think about ourselves and other people. It can deepen our understanding of the purpose of existence. It can free us to think more honestly about the consequences of our own choices and actions. It can certainly transform the way we value life or regard and think about death.

Those tangible, transformative benefits of prayer may accelerate or deepen a personal relationship with God. But, again, they won't depend on such a relationship. Inspiration pours toward us in unlimited ways. The prayers in this collection show that. And the unconditionally compassionate and sacred Buddhist prayers that I treasure in these pages exemplify it particularly well.

Asher is a Buddhist meditation teacher who grew up in an accomplished, competitive, secular Jewish family. Now in his late thirties, he made a strikingly clear statement to me quite recently about his commitment to prayer. "By praying to the outer Buddha or the bodhisattvas [enlightened beings], I know that I am awakening the inner Buddha, my own Buddha [eternal] nature." He went on, "What that means for me is changing the atmosphere within myself and beyond. I do this both through the power of prayer itself, and through what I pay attention to and give myself to."

Vanessa is another friend, closer to my own age and with a keen interest in poetry and literature. She describes herself as having little or no sense of religion or spirituality, and certainly no conventional belief in God or, indeed, the power of prayer. Nevertheless, she was keen to read this book in manuscript and reported back that just reading the prayers soothed her. Was this a spiritual experience? I would say yes. What's more, it was also a sensual experience, because even as Vanessa spoke to me about it, she was also telling me how her body felt easier and more relaxed as she read, and how she had held the pages of the manuscript close to her body like, in her words, "letters from a friend."

I am touched by the tenderness that Vanessa expressed, and I'm keenly aware that when people tell me of illnesses, grief or losses that are shadowing their lives and I say, "I will pray for you," or, "I will remember you and your family in my prayers," they are invariably grateful. This is not because they assume my prayers are more effective than anyone else's but because the promise to be "held in prayer" offers unfailing comfort. It is a *felt* experience, and one that many people hunger to know better.

It's also a reminder of our part in others' well-being. Prayer centered on and expressive of love is unifying. It transcends differences, even while it respects them. It teaches us the truth of our interdependence. And that both the world and our vision of it are greater than anything we can routinely imagine. *"Every fear falls away as we enter into . . . Thy glory of love,"* taught Unity Church founders Cora and Charles Fillmore.

One of my most crucial discoveries through prayer is also the simplest: "I am not alone." Praying, I join my heart, mind and highest intentions with those of countless others. At the very same time, I can listen as well as speak to the "small, quiet voice within": the "voice" of soul or spirit. Through prayer, I experience the eternal dimensions as profound mystery and also profound intimacy.

. . .

The twentieth-century Quaker writer Thomas H. Jeavons conjures up the widening circles of influence that prayer creates with these words: "When we pray we affirm our hope and intention of coming closer to God. We work to deepen our trust in and love for God . . . As we pray and change in this relationship we become better equipped to be instruments of God's love."

To become "instruments of love" is the highest ambition to which you or I can aspire, and it is available to all. It need not depend on privilege, education or religion. It depends only on perspective, will, and a quiet conviction that the part each of us plays in our shared world truly matters.

By refining our thoughts and intentions, prayer helps profoundly with this. A life secured by prayer brings hope, possibility and comfort. It brings vital insight. It makes the world new each day.

That's the message in these profound words from the eighteenth-century Jewish mystic Ba'al Shem Tov: *"The world is new to us every morning. This is God's gift. And every person should believe that they are reborn each day."*

Prayer is itself our means of renewal, or rebirth. As the sun rises, so can our thoughts and intentions. As the sun sets, so our thoughts and intentions can settle and be deepened.

Collecting many of these prayers over years, and adapting, translating and writing others, I have prayed for inspiration. Prayer *is* inspiration, or it can be. As I have prayed, written and made my choices, I wanted to be sure that every one of these prayers could also inspire you, lift your spirits, give back to you a vision of yourself that's authentically hopeful, and that's unconditionally connected with life, rather than distanced from it.

My greatest prayer is that each of us will come to recognize the power we have to contribute to a kinder, fairer and more loving world. That's the world in which we will find our greatest happiness. Whatever their source, these are prayers that support that sacred vision.

When I pray, I reap the benefits. Yet as I pray—and in all the different ways that I pray—I can't keep those benefits to myself. That would make no sense. Prayer changes me for the better. (And never mind that I have so far to go! Some of those difficulties are new prompts to pray.) Prayer changes my inner world. I am quite sure that it heals, and loves into healing, the outer world also.

Bringing together these prayers, I see what a vital resource prayer has been, and is, in my own complex life. I simply do not know how I would have moved through the most difficult times without prayer, or fully treasured the bliss of the most joyful times, or valued precious "ordinary" life.

Over my lifetime so far, I have lived in six different countries and visited many others. I have prayed, worshipped, chanted, sung and sat in contemplative or meditative silence in countless different situations, from ashrams in India, Shinto and Buddhist shrines and temples in Japan, synagogues in Israel and Australia, outdoor Mass and cathedral Evensong in Hawaii, African-American Pentecostal churches in Alabama, Louisiana and Tennessee, ordination services in New York's Saint John the Divine (including my own), countless small and large churches in France, Sufi *zikr* gatherings in London and Sydney, Maori and Aboriginal ceremonies in New Zealand and Australia, days-long Buddhist, Christian and interfaith retreats, and more churches and temples than I can recall.

It's my great fortune to feel at home wherever there is a spirit of love and inclusion. I have led spiritually inclusive retreats for over twenty years and similarly inclusive services for a large, inner-city congregation for over seven years. As a former practicing therapist, too, I have discovered for myself what drives people apart as well as what brings them to a new knowing of their spiritual nature and power.

In their variety, the prayers in this book reflect my lifetime's eager exposure to the world's faiths and religious cultures, as well as my Christian formation within both the Catholic and Protestant streams. In their unity, the prayers in this book reflect my stubborn belief in the goodness that each of us is capable of realizing: the peaceful encounters, the goodwill, cooperation, forgiveness, praise, recovery, reconciliation, gratitude, kindness, fairness and deep comfort that would, truly, bring heaven to earth.

Some of these prayers are in my own words, and reflect our twenty-first-century needs as well as language. Others are my carefully re-thought translations or respectful adaptations of other writers' prayers, including writers of the world's most enduring scriptures, who have probably been more extensively and diversely translated and "re-scribed" than writers of any other kind. It has been a particular joy to work with those timeless words and the intentions they offer. And there are many prayers here, too, given to you much as they were first written or recorded, whether that was within the last year or two, or millennia ago. Some are more like succinct teachings or messages than prayers; some are meditative; some ask for more robust sharing. All are offered with care for how they will "land" in your mind and heart.

In the ancient words of the Tao Te Ching: *"What is well planted cannot be uprooted. . . ."* However ancient or new these prayers, their "planting" depends on your welcome.

How to Pray

Prayer is not just something that you *do*; it quickly becomes part of who you are. For many people, it's central to who they are. That's true for me, even when I am not formally praying or haven't been on my knees or a meditation cushion for hours or days.

To discover this, though, prayer itself must become your teacher. And what a generous teacher prayer can be! But learning as you pray may first mean unshackling prayer from dreary notions of duty, effort, piety or perfection.

It may also mean shaking up some old assumptions: that prayer is primarily about praising God or bargaining for a better deal; that there's a perfect way to pray that's passed you by; that only weak people pray; that prayers must be answered precisely and quickly or are a waste of time; that your faith's or denomination's prayers are more legitimate or pleasing to God than everyone else's; that only convinced theists pray; that there's plenty of time to discover prayer when the important business of life is completed.

I'm not mocking those assumptions—or only a little. Nor, though, do I want them to delay you from discovering what each treasure of a prayer in this book can give you *if you are willing to make yourself available.*

We often think of prayer as something that we do (or ought to, if only we had the time). Yet prayer gives itself to us. It creates time as it renews us. It also strengthens us. It reminds us that we are not alone. It can soothe us. It can certainly inspire us. That famous wish from the movie *Star Wars*, "May the force be with you," sums up prayer gloriously for me. It is a force. And it can be with us! How beautiful then to know that we can wish that for others, and for ourselves.

As you begin to pray more regularly, and perhaps with a greater sense of adventure, you will discover that the words of any prayer are only the beginning. Prayer is about listening as much as speaking, and about receiving as much as asking. And all that reverberates long after formal praying stops.

Any prayer worth praying offers a message of love, sometimes one first given in that particular form many centuries ago, perhaps in a country far from yours. But geographical, temporal and even cultural differences don't count for much when it comes to prayer. Prayer unites us, not just at this time but also across time. This means that you can quite easily receive a prayer as though it were written yesterday, or this morning.

Your part is to seek, to stay open and to be receptive. It's also to surrender your expectations as much as you dare, allowing the prayer's words and silences to hold you, or to take you where you need to go.

And while prayer is usually shared through words, there are many other ways to live prayerfully, including service to others, spiritual study, caring for the physical world, sending good wishes, holding the hand of a vulnerable stranger, speaking up for fairness, listening deeply, appreciating what you have, finding new courage in the face of suffering, or celebrating the details of everyday life with greater joy.

During the intense time when I was finishing this book, I wrote words on my public Facebook page that were and were not a prayer. The response was heartfelt and immediate: "Well past 11 p.m. and I've been finishing little household chores that didn't get done earlier—and feeling just awed and moved by the so-called 'ordinariness' of this day. How lucky are we when we have safe homes, clean sheets, water in the tap, food in the fridge, and quiet inside and out? So much gratitude for every bit of it."

On another morning recently, I woke with the clear sound of my friend, musician Elizabeth Lecoanet, singing "Nearer My God to Thee." This was gloriously familiar and odd simultaneously, because Elizabeth has sung, in my company, "God be in my head" (and God *was* in my head!), but not "Nearer. . . ." Our minds can quite obviously be a veritable treasure house of prayer, and playful, instructive and creative with it.

This easy diversity of prayerful forms is freeing as well as encouraging. It ends the illusion that there is only one way to pray, or only one source of prayers that is legitimate.

Prayers that console, encourage, ask or praise are, nonetheless, what most of us associate with praying. There are many such prayers here. I use them, too. As you choose and pray them, you are likely to hear their messages gratefully, especially as you return to them, making them your own.

Other "prayers" in these pages are more like poems or even seeds: brief teachings laden with potential to shift your view, or to bring your mind closer to an appreciation of the sacred nature of life itself. They will help you develop a willingness to reflect and contemplate: superb acts of prayer. They may also be what you take with you into a time of meditation or journal writing.

The variety of prayers here means that your breadth of mood and need can be met. I am hoping that you will quite often make your choices instinctively, bringing to your selection a sense of adventure as well as deepening trust.

Whether the prayers are new to you or cherished and familiar, I am quite sure that praying—like music—is best experienced in the present moment. Anticipating a time of prayer can be wonderful, but what's nourishing is to *experience* prayer . . . to find the prayer you need and to discover its particular meaning for *this* day, especially as your familiarity with prayer increases. Prayer may even become your "default" thinking, as one elderly man expressed it. "Even when I am thinking about something else, I'm still praying," he said. "And when I am not thinking about something else, I observe that my mind shifts toward the company of the Divine."

For you it may be different. Prayer for you may be a few snatched moments before you throw yourself into the urgencies of the day. It may be something you turn to only in extreme need. And I can understand that. Yet I also hope that the rewards of regular prayer and of tuning the mind prayerfully become much clearer to you as you use this book. And this is a book I long for you to *use*—in the very midst of living.

BEFORE YOU PRAY

The minutes or seconds when you are choosing to pray are integral to prayer itself. That is when you engage your spirit and will, using thought to do so. It is when you affirm through your choice to turn inward that life is sacred and that what we call "life" and "mind" extend beyond yourself, beyond cognitive mind and mortal body. Anticipating prayer, you align yourself with wisdom and love across and beyond time. It is also when you invite in the mystery that we call prayer and allow yourself to be prayer's instrument.

PRAY IN THE PRESENT MOMENT

Come to each prayer freshly, even if you have known it since child-hood. Let it meet you as you are now, today. Setting aside your pre-conceptions, you will experience surprises and new depths. *"All things bright and beautiful,"* may be a cheerful phrase from childhood, but what poignancy it can have in your older years, when suffering and forgiveness have marked your life. Let yourself imagine that your chosen prayer has been written for you this very day—even when it is ancient. *"May everything I do be what you would wish for me, O Lord."* Receive the words as you would any gift, with gratitude.

MAKE THE PRAYERS YOUR OWN

Let the words of the prayer become yours. When a prayer feels mean-ingful or calls out to you, write it out in your own handwriting. Learn it by heart or take just a single phrase and infuse it with the power of a mantra. Write your old and new favorites on cards, in notebooks or a journal. Send them to friends. Create love letters to the sacred out of them. Draw them or paint them. Sing them or dance them. Whisper them into the dark at night and call them out loud to the sky by day. Trust that the prayers that are most needed and most "yours" will write themselves across your heart if you allow that. When I am most needy, my prayers have virtually no words at all. Often, that's my deepest praying.

CHECK WHAT MOTIVATES YOU

Whatever drives or inspires you to pray will also determine how prayer can work on you and support you. It's quite usual for your motivation to mature and change, even from day to day. As I write this, however, I am also thinking of Persian Sufi poet Hafiz's famous phrase, "I am happy before I have reason," and how easily it becomes "I am praying—and am *prayed*—before I have a reason. . . ."

CHOOSE YOUR PRAYERS SPONTANEOUSLY

Choose with trust and a light heart the prayer that will accompany you through any particular day or situation. Each prayer and teaching in this collection brings to you a message of wisdom, courage, forgiveness, generosity, appreciation, unity or love. This message can inspire and carry you, perhaps even through your darkest hours. *"Love is perfected within us." "Oneness of life and light . . ." "Come, comforter of my soul . . ." "Let our lives bring heaven to earth."*

LET INSTINCT GUIDE YOU

Perhaps you will choose a prayer because it is familiar, but at least sometimes let instinct or intuition guide you. Trust yourself to be adventurous in your choosing. Opening this book, and discovering your prayer for the day randomly, is seldom random! And no prayer with an authentic message of wisdom, compassion, courage or love is ever "wrong." When your eyes "land" on a prayer, don't spend time wondering, "Why this one?" Read it, pray it, absorb it, live it. Give thanks for it, and for what it brings.

PRAYING PRAYERS

When does reading, whispering, speaking or sharing words *become* praying? Readying the body can help, but it's not enough. I want to return to the idea of "tuning" so that listening inwardly becomes as inevitable as speaking. Surrender also comes to mind: turning your attention away from the clamorous superficialities to the depths of existence. Spaciousness is next, and is no small thing. When we worry chronically, as many do, we block our strength. When we pray, we free strength, imagination and vision. We make room for hope. We make room for reconciliation and resurrection. We see from the inside out. *"The light of your body is your eye. When your eye sees clearly, your entire being is illuminated."* Reception is central, too: receiving the words of the prayer and the shift in energy and atmosphere that praying and being prayed may allow, extending trust away from your small self to Self, to soul, to spirit, to the unnameable, intimate, infinite creative power that is the Ground of Being and Love.

BEYOND WORDS

However beautiful they are and however inspiring, the words of a prayer are no more than a container for the wordless energy that the prayer evokes or liberates. That sounds mysterious, yet when you give yourself the chance to sit with the prayer in silence after you read or pray it, you will experience it taking you beyond words. Whenever you can, allow for some minutes of silence as your mind and feelings "rest" with the prayer, and transcend it. Take the "emptiness" around any prayer, including the literal space on these pages or in your journal, as well as the space you are offering prayer in your own mind, as an invitation to the fullness that silence brings.

COMMIT TO PRAYER

Steadfastness in prayer is as rewarding as commitment is in any other relationship. It frees you from the need constantly to decide whether you *feel* like praying, if prayer is "worth your time," or if you are getting from it what you "have to have." Pray because you can. Let the rewards of prayer emerge as they will. Surrender to what is. *"Deep in their roots, all flowers keep the light."* What reassurance there is in those few words! Trust that any arid times will pass; so will any lightning strikes of bliss or ecstasy. Discover steadiness. *"Those who are good, I treat as good. Those who are not good, I treat as good. In this way I discover goodness."* What will not fail you is the quiet accumulation of meaning, purpose, company, consolation and salvation.

PRAY OFTEN

Set aside the thought that prayer is an obligation. It is not. Celebrate your freedom to pray—and to receive whatever prayer gives. Although praying only when you are most desperate or have most to celebrate is how many discover prayer's power, it's an opportunity missed *not* to pray, whatever your mood or need. Prayer has its best chance to work for you and on you when your early thoughts of the day are prayerful, even if you are not formally praying, and when your evenings end in much the same way. To enter the zone of timelessness that's prayer takes little time! You can radically increase your own well-being and benefit others when you bookend your days with prayer, when you choose prayer rather than frustration or anxiety in challenging moments, when you meet life hopefully and with gratitude as well as trust.

May my mind open,
releasing judgments and interpretations.
May my life open,
releasing expectations,
so that I may embrace what is
and see it truly.

PRAY WITH OTHERS

"Where two or three are gathered together in my name, there am I in the midst of them." This is a profound teaching attributed to Jesus. It sublimely accentuates the atmosphere and energy present when people pray collectively. Quakers, who worship with few or no words, call it "gathered silence." Shared prayer can bridge differences and put those differences in their place. The simple, familiar words, "Let us pray," are already reassuring. When leading prayers, I sometimes use the words, "Join with me as I pray . . ." It is that *joining* that is almost magical in its power to unite and comfort, especially when we think of prayer itself as a vital and vitalizing act of communion and care.

PRAY ALONE

Praying when you are alone can bring tremendous inner stability, peace and comfort. The relief of discovering, as we pray, that we are *not* alone is scarcely lessened if you don't "believe" in a personal God. Prayer is the language of the ineffable, the holy or sacred. It transcends both form and dogma. It is simultaneously a reaching *out* and a reaching *in* that takes you into the heart's deepest knowing. Praying alone we may discover an uncluttered freedom to *be*. When I wake in the night or in the morning, and as I am going to sleep, I tune my mind with simple prayer. At other times, the desire to pray itself becomes prayer, a door opening to deeper reflection than I could otherwise achieve.

IN TIMES OF GREAT NEED

Our first instinct may be to surround a difficult or desperate situation with anxious thoughts. In doing so, and despite our best intentions, we add tension to tension. An immensely positive alternative is steadily and persistently to send prayer or positive wishes for the highest good to prevail. Or to pray evoking the strengths needed: *"I am now facing this situation with loving kindness and trust in each coming moment . . ."* *"May we all be well and happy."* *"I open to the truth of love, seen and unseen."* That subtle action is always inwardly healing, whatever the external outcome. I will frequently surround difficult situations with divine light, creating a picture patiently in my mind of golden or white light fully embracing and holding all concerned. Sometimes I add to this a picture of enlightened beings or angels supporting me or others. Or I consciously evoke an awareness of myself as soul, and all others as souls. This, too, is praying.

HEAR THE CALLS TO PRAY

Listening to the "small, still voice within" is one of the most profound forms of prayer. When I offer prayer guidance on retreats it is at least as much about listening to the silence that precedes and follows formal prayer as it is to absorbing the words of the prayers and to what they offer and allow. Nonetheless, an external call to prayer is powerfully effective. In some traditions, the call to prayer is already the beginning of praying. The striking of meditation bells is also familiar and so are the gestures of the body: kneeling, sitting or standing still so that the mind can settle, joining hands at the heart, or placing them upward on your thighs, bowing your head, closing your eyes and turning inward and affirming: *This matters.*

VALUE THE MIRACLE

I have already called prayer *teacher, mystery, adventure, reward, friend, relationship* and especially *answer*. Now I want to go further. Prayer is also a miracle that is constantly unfolding. Participating in prayer, we move more deeply into life. We experience at first hand life's spaciousness and its sacred dimensions. We discover the choice we have about who we are becoming, and also how this affects others and influences and creates our world. We discover that we belong unconditionally to something far greater than ourselves—however variously we might describe this.

Praying with others, praying alone, just praying, we become who and what we were born to be. We become ourselves.

Let our love flow outward through the universe:
to its height, its depth and its breadth.
Let this be an unlimited love, free from any trace of hatred or enmity.

While we stand or walk, sit or lie down,
as long as we are awake and free from indifference,
let us strive for this with a one-pointed mind.
Let our lives bring heaven to earth.

PRAYERS IN
DAILY LIFE

There is no more powerful way to support yourself in daily life than to pray, and to experience the strength, hope and comfort that prayer gives. Repeating familiar prayers or enjoying new ones; expressing your gratitude for the gifts of the day; asking for whatever insight or help is needed; offering blessings; sharing prayers with others, or beginning and ending your day with the stillness that comes with prayer, you are reconnecting to life's deepest meaning. And, with ease and trust, you are drawing strength from that meaning.

Prayer is never *outside* everyday life. It is part of it, and can be part of you. Every act and action within your life can be suffused with prayerful intentions. In fact, to pray in and around those "ordinary moments" of everyday existence is to bring the sacred home, quite literally.

Making time for prayer means making time for your own self: not just your efficient, money-earning, household-running, ever-busy self, but *all* of who you are, including your highest intentions, your heart, spirit, soul.

And there's more. Allowing prayer to begin, end and permeate your days, you are setting your inner compass in the direction of love. You are opening to sacred inspiration. As this becomes a quiet constant in your life, you are far less likely to feel helpless, even in times of confusion. When those feelings do arise, you can meet them courageously.

This is because prayer sustains you from the inside out. It helps others, too, because prayer lifts the atmosphere around you as well as within you.

Praying—whether alone or with other people—also gives you a much-needed chance to affirm a world that's not entirely dictated by external concerns. We know how seductive external goals and demands can be. We also know how rarely they bring lasting contentment and peace.

In this section I have included some particularly lovely prayers that will appeal to children as much as adults. The prayers we learn to say in childhood may bring us comfort long after our vision of "God" or prayer itself has matured. Prayer is one of the most beautiful resources that families or communities can draw upon, making differences or antagonisms far less important than the life and hopes we share.

Any prayer or short teaching in this collection can enhance your daily life and steady you. The more familiar you are with a particular prayer or reading, the more its inner meaning will reveal itself to you—and be revealed through you.

Take a few moments to write out any prayer that seems to "speak" to you. Say it often. Share it. Let its music ring in your ears and heart. Let its thinking become yours.

Come to me all you who struggle and are burdened.
Come to me and I will give you rest.
Take my yoke and learn from my example.
In me you will find courage and humility of heart.
In the deepest reaches of your souls, you will find rest.
For my yoke is gentle, my burden is light.

—*Matthew 11:28–30*

Holy One, you are beyond simple knowing;
I praise you with unceasing wonder.
You are wrapped in light like a cloak.
You stretch out the sky like a curtain . . .
You walk on the wings of the wind . . .
. . . I will sing to you at every moment.
With every breath I will praise you.
May I transcend selfishness.
May you shine always from my heart.

—*Adapted from Psalm 104:1–3, 33*

Lord, give me a full heart
so that with gratitude I can empty myself.
Lord, give me *life*,
so that I can lavish it
in service for the world.

—*Ansari*

Sitting quietly, turning inward, I think
of the Being of Light,
the One who is Supreme in love and peace,
purity, wisdom and joy.
In the presence of the Supreme,
I feel the comfort and security of being surrounded
by God's light.

Resting in this moment, I stay connected
with this light,
and it's as though God's truth,
God's mercy,
is reaching the roots of my being,
making me strong.

And as I feel the warmth of God's love,
my heart opens.
I become able to share fragrance and beauty
with the world.

—B. K. SISTER JAYANTI

The fruits of the Spirit are love,
joy, peace, resilience, gentleness,
goodness, courage, humility and restraint.
There is no power greater than these qualities.

—GALATIANS 5:22–23

Blessed is the Source,
out of which all being
has emerged.

—Morning prayer, Jewish tradition

Blessed are You,
Lord our God,
King of the universe,
who takes away
sleep from my eyes
and slumber from
my eyelids.

—Morning prayer, Jewish tradition

It's morning! O Lord our God,
who has chased the sleep from our eyes.
We ask you to accept our prayers and give us
confidence and love.
Bless our coming in and our going out,
our thoughts, words and actions.
Let us begin our day by praising the sweetness
of your kindness.
Hallowed be thy name!
May your kingdom come!

—Adapted from the liturgy of
the Greek church, c. AD 300

As I wake, let my mind open to the gifts
of each new day,
and give thanks.

Let me wake to the presence of Love.
Let me wake to any gifts of Spirit that I may
need today:
joy, peace, resilience, gentleness,
goodness, courage, humility, restraint.

Let me face the day with confidence
and quiet trust.

The "I" who moves through this day is
more than body,
more than feelings, thoughts;
the "I" who moves through this day is all those,
and eternally more.
I am capable of freedom.
I am capable of choice.

Soul of souls,
Holy Spirit,
Beloved:
I am not alone.
Let me give thanks.
Blessed be.

—*S.D.*

The first thing we have to find out is the kind of practice
that suits *our* souls—
ours, not someone else's, and
now, at this stage
of our soul's growth.

—*EVELYN UNDERHILL*

Look to this day.
For it is life.
The very life of life.
In its brief course lie all
the realities and truths of existence.
The bliss of growth.
The splendor of action.
The glory of power.
For yesterday is now a dream.
Tomorrow is just a vision.
But today, when lived well,
makes every yesterday a
dream of happiness.
And every tomorrow,
a vision of hope.

—*SALUTATION TO THE SUN, SANSKRIT PROVERB*

O Lord,
we ask that you will make
the door of this church, and of our lives,
wide enough to receive all who need human love and fellowship,
and the care of Divine love.

We ask that you will make the door
narrow enough to shut out all
envy, pride, indifference and hate.

Make its threshold
smooth enough to be
no stumbling block for children,
nor to straying or reluctant feet . . .
Make this a gateway to our knowledge of eternity.
May we bring heaven to earth.

—*Bishop Thomas Ken*

How should we love Him?
I say that God asks of us that just as He loved us
without any second thoughts, so (in that same way)
He should be loved by us.
In what way can we do this then?
I tell you, through a means which He has established
by which we can love Him freely.
That is, we can be useful, not to Him, which is impossible,
but to our neighbors.
To show the love that we have for Him,
we ought to serve and love every creature
and extend our kindness to good and bad,
as much to one who does us ill service and criticizes us,
as to one who treats us well.
For His love extends to all.

—*Catherine of Siena*

Before the bread, the wheat.
Before the wheat, the grain.
Before the grain, the sun and rain,
and beauty of God's love.

—GRACE BEFORE MEALS

For family, friends and food,
for earth, sky, air
and the miracle of seeds, sun and water,
for those who hoe and pick and pack,
and those who plan and shop and cook,
we join hands around our table today
and with a single voice we say,
"Thank you, Lord!"

—S.D.

Food is the gift of the whole universe: earth, sky and
much hard work.
May we live in a way that is worthy of this food.
May we transform our unskillful states of mind,
especially greed.
May we eat only foods that nourish us and
prevent illness.
May we accept this food for the realization of
understanding and love.

—ADAPTED FROM THICH NHAT HANH

Sh'ma Yisra'el
Adonai eloheinu
Adonai ehad

Hear O Israel,
the Lord is our God.
The Lord is One.

Love the Lord your God
with all your heart
with all your soul
with all your might.

—Deuteronomy 6:4

Within God's hand,
I lay my soul,
both when I sleep
and when I wake,
and with my soul,
my body too.
My Lord is close.
I need not be afraid.

—Traditional Jewish evening prayer

Now I lay me down to sleep
I pray to God my soul to keep.
Stay close with me throughout the night.
Wake me fresh with morning's light.

God bless you!
God bless me!
God bless *all* who dwell with Thee!
Amen

—*Adapted Christian prayer*

Angel of God,
my guardian dear,
to whom God's love,
commits me here.
Ever this day [or night]
be at my side,
to light and guard,
to rule and guide.
Amen

—*Traditional Catholic prayer*

There is no fear in love.
Perfect love casts out fear.
Fear brings torment with it.
Those who feel tormented have
yet to discover love.

—*1 John 4:18*

It's not bread alone that lets you live.
It's the words that come from the mouth of God.

When you pray, say:
Father, Mother, Birther of all,
Your very name is holy.
May Heaven come to Earth.
Give us each day the nourishment that we need.
Forgive us our wrongdoings,
as we ourselves must forgive those who have wronged us.
Save us from our greatest difficulties.

Ask. It will be given.
Seek. You will find.
Knock. The door will be opened for you.

—WORDS OF JESUS CHRIST, MATTHEW 4:4; 6:9–13; 7:7

You are precious in my eyes,
and honored,
and I love you.

Do not be afraid,
for I am with you.
From wherever you come,
I will lead you home.

—ISAIAH 43:4, 5

Let me first turn my attention to my own existence
and pray:
May I be well and happy.
May I be free from suffering, unhappiness, and anger.
May I be free from sadness.
May my body be strong and healthy.
May I be filled with loving kindness.
May I be peaceful and content.

Now let me think of the people I know best:
family . . . friends . . . colleagues . . . teachers . . . neighbors . . .
Sending them profound good wishes I ask:
May they be well and happy.
May they be free from suffering, unhappiness, and anger.
May they be free from sadness.
May they be strong and healthy.
May they be filled with loving kindness.
May they be peaceful and content.

Now let me think about all the people I don't know,
We share this planet together.
They want to be happy, like I do.
They want to feel safe, like I do.
They are part of my human family.
Sending them profound good wishes I ask:
May they be well and happy.
May they be free from suffering, unhappiness, and anger.
May they be free from sadness.
May they be strong and healthy.
May they be filled with loving kindness.
May they be peaceful and content.

Now let me think about all the people whose views disturb me.
Or whose actions I despise.
We share this planet together.
They want to be happy, like I do.
They want to feel safe, like I do.
Like them, hate them: they too are part of my human family.
Their intentions affect me.
My intentions affect them.
Sending them profound good wishes I ask:
May they be well and happy.
May they be free from suffering, unhappiness, and anger.
May they be free from sadness.
May they be strong and healthy.
May they be filled with loving kindness.
May they be peaceful and content.

Finally I will think about the animals, birds, insects and fish,
all creatures living in the air, on the earth and in the oceans.
Sending them good wishes I ask:
May they be well and happy.
May they be free.
May they live safely.

Finally:
I send all beings loving kindness from my heart.
I open my heart to receive loving kindness from all beings.

—Inspired by the Metta Sutta

How to meditate?
Bring yourself back to the point quite gently.

And even if you do nothing during the whole of your hour but
bring your heart back a thousand times,
though it went away every time you brought it back,
your hour would be very well employed.

—*Francis de Sales*

May my words be in harmony with my thinking,
and may my thinking be in harmony with my words,
O Lord of Love.

Let me realize you in my awareness.
Let me realize the truth of the sacred teachings.
Let me translate that truth in my daily living.

May I affirm the truth of the sacred teachings.
May I speak what is true.
May the truth protect me.
And may it protect those who guide me.

OM *shanti, shanti, shanti*
[peace, peace, peace].

—*Adapted from the Aitareya Upanishad*

Join me as I pray:
Divine Friend, Holy Spirit,
whom we know and name
in many different ways:

We ask that you bless us as
we open to the richness of our lives.
Help us to understand how
the sublime beauty of your love
reflects the beauty of our souls.

We are mindful of you,
Soul of souls, Home to all:
we are mindful of all you have given us.
We are mindful of the earth and its bounty.
We are mindful of one another.

In your faithful presence,
and in the presence of one another,
we open to the qualities
that we most want to nourish and express.
We are ready for that.

We also recall the habits or tendencies
that we most want to curtail or transform.
We are ready for that.

We welcome the seeds of possibility
that we choose now to nurture.
And yes, we are ready.

In your faithful presence,
and in the presence of one another,
our lives can blossom into wholeness.
We can share your abundance.
Blessed be.

—S.D.

O great Spirit,
Help me to speak the truth quietly.
Help me to listen with an open mind
when other people speak.
Help me to remember the peace that
is to be found in silence.

—*Traditional Cherokee prayer*

Lord you called to me
And I did only answer thee
With words slow and sleepy:
"Wait a while! Wait a while!"

But while and while have no end,
And "wait a while" is a long road.

—*14th-century English poem*

Before I ask . . .
let me give thanks.

For the gifts I have,
for the mistakes I have already made,
for the experiences I have learned from,
for the insights I can trust,
for the friends I can turn to,
for the words I can find,
for the constancy of Spirit,
let me give thanks.

—*S.D.*

Whatever extends through the universe,
I regard as my body,
and whatever directs the universe,
I regard as my nature.

All people are my brothers and sisters,
and all things are my companions.

—CHANG-TSAI

Any offering is acceptable to me—
leaf, flower, fruit, water—
when it is given with a loving heart.

Whatever you do,
make it an offering to me.
Whatever you say, eat, pray, offer,
whatever you endure,
make it an offering to me.

—BHAGAVAD GITA 9:26–27

Whether you eat or drink,
or whatever you do,
do it in such a way
that the Divine can be revealed through it.

—1 CORINTHIANS 10:31

Come, O Creator Spirit, come!
Welcome to you, beloved Friend.
Fill all the hearts that you have made.
Come, Spirit, stay!

—*"Veni, Creator Spiritus"*

Lord, this heart of mine is your temple.
These actions of mine are your handmaidens.
This body of mine is your home.
My senses testify to you.
My sleep rests in you.
My feet walk your journey.
My words are prayers.
Oh Lord, all that I say,
all that I do,
is worship.

—*Shankara*

Love can certainly be difficult.
Because to love is not enough.
We must, like God, become love.

—*Angelus Silesius*

You shouldn't wait until God comes to you
and says, 'I am.'
A god who parades his strengths
is meaningless.
You must know that God blows through you
from the beginning,
and when your heart burns within and betrays nothing,
then know that God is working there.

—RAINER MARIA RILKE
(TRANSLATED BY MARK S. BURROWS)

We come as little children
into the sacred and trustful presence of Thy love,
knowing full well that only love can draw and hold us
in peace and harmony and prosperity.
Every fear falls away as we enter into Thee
and Thy glory of love
and as we bask in the sunshine of love,
Thy love,
Thy never-failing love!

—CHARLES AND CORA FILLMORE

O God, You are my mother,
my father, my brother, my friend.
You are all that I know.
You are all that I have.
You are everything to me,
God of gods!

—"TWAMEVA MATA," HINDU CHANT

So shall no part of day or night
From sacredness be free;
But all my life, in every step,
Be fellowship with Thee.

—*Horatius Bonar*

Thanks be to you, dear Lord,
For all the benefits you have given me.
And for the sorrows you have taken from me.
O most kind Redeemer, friend and brother,
day by day of Thee three things I pray:
To see thee more clearly;
To love thee more dearly;
To follow thee more nearly,
day by day.

—*Attributed to Richard of Chichester*

Do we not have just a single Father?
Did not just one God create us all?
Why then does humankind deal treacherously
with one another?
This betrays the teachings of our ancestors.

—*Malachi 2:10*

Let me seek goodness.
And find it.
Let me seek kindness.
And return it.
Let me seek hope.
And express it.
Let me seek compassion.
And receive it.
Let me seek wisdom.
And recognize it.
Let me seek fidelity.
And honor it.
Let me seek forgiveness.
And offer it.
Let me seek gentleness.
And treasure it.
Let me seek patience.
And nourish it.
Let me seek joy.
And delight in it.
Let me seek courage.
And share it.
Let me seek generosity.
And prize it.
Let me seek tolerance.
And emulate it.
Let me seek love.
And live it.

—S.D.

Those who are good, I treat as good.
Those who are not good, I treat as good.
In so doing, I discover goodness.

—*Tao Te Ching, Vs. 49*

Dear God, you are my most constant friend.
You are there for me always.
Help me to remember you
as the faithful friend that you are.
With me in joy.
With me in sorrow.
With me.
Help me also to be a true friend to others.
Help me to be a true friend to myself.

—*S.D.*

Standing on the bare ground,
my head bathed by the blithe air,
and uplifted into infinite space—
all mean egotism vanishes.
I become a transparent eyeball.
I am nothing.
I see all.
The currents of the Universal Being
circulate through me.
I am a particle of God.

—*Ralph Waldo Emerson*

May everything I say,
May everything I think,
May everything I do
be what you would wish for me,
O Lord,
My rock and redeemer.

—*Psalm 19:14*

Holiness is the highest good.
It is also the source of our contentment.
Happy is the one who commits without reserve to
the sacred adventure.

—*Adapted from Zoroastrian "Ashem Vohu"*

Waking is itself a blessing.
As are my eyes to see.
My ears to hear.
My nose to follow.
My limbs to take me where I need to go.
My hands, to offer and receive.
My tongue, mouth, lips to taste and praise.
And all the time, heart beating.
Breath breathing.
Life living.
Awareness of Love
changing everything.

—*S.D.*

Love God.
Thrust down pride.
Forgive gladly.
Be sober in eating and drinking.
Find honest company.
Reverence thine elders.
Trust in God's mercy.
Be well occupied.
Do not waste time.
Falling down, despair not.
Ever take a fresh, new, good purpose.
Persevere constantly.
Wash clean.
Awake promptly.
Enrich yourself with positive acts.
Learn diligently.
Teach what you have learned, lovingly.

—JOHN COLET

As a skilful leader,
you lead without any sense of urgency.
You stand up for what's right
without anger.
You remain modest.
Doing that,
you bring out the best in other people.

—TAO TE CHING, VS. 68

In the beginning was the Word.
And the Word was with God.
And the Word was God.
. . . In him was life.
And the life was the light for all.

—*John 1:1–2, 4*

Hari OM. In the beginning, Spirit was One.
The entire universe was Spirit.
Nothing else saw.
Spirit said: "From my Being, I will make all the worlds."
All worlds were made including space, the world of light;
earth, the world of living and dying; oceans and waters.
Then Spirit said: "I see these worlds and will make
caretakers for these worlds."
Out of the waters Spirit gathered guardians,
gave them form and life,
and entered into them through the door called bliss.

Adapted from Aitareya Upanishad 1:2–3

All the avoidable suffering in the world
comes from seeking pleasure only for oneself.
All the attainable happiness in the world
comes from seeking pleasure for others.

As no one wants to endure the smallest suffering
nor ever has enough of happiness,
there is no difference between myself and other people.
So let me make others peaceful and happy.

May those who are weakened by cold find warmth.
May those who are oppressed by heat be cooled.
May the infinite waters that pour
from the great clouds of the Enlightened Ones
refresh all beings.
May the torrents of lava and blazing stones
become a rain of flowers.
May those who have no clothes or shelter
find what they need.
May those who are hungry find food.
May those who are thirsty find water.
May those who are unsafe find safety.

May those who are fearful lose their fears.
May those who are bound be free.
May the powerless find the true meaning of power.
May people wake up to the joys that come as they benefit others.

For as long as space endures,
for as long as living beings remain on this earth,
I vow
to dispel suffering and bring joy to the world.

—*Shantideva*

There was a time when meadow, grove, and stream,
The earth, and every common sight,
To me did seem
Apparelled in celestial light,
The glory and the freshness of a dream . . .

Our birth is but a sleep and a forgetting:
The Soul that rises with us, our Life's Star,
Hath had elsewhere its setting,
And cometh from afar:
Not in entire forgetfulness,
And not in utter nakedness,
But trailing clouds of glory do we come
From God, who is our home.

—WILLIAM WORDSWORTH, IN "INTIMATIONS OF IMMORTALITY"

Sleep my child and peace attend thee,
all through the night.
Guardian angels God will send thee,
all through the night.
Soft the drowsy hours are creeping,
hill and vale in slumber sleeping,
I my loved ones' watch am keeping,
all through the night.

—LULLABY SUNG TO TRADITIONAL WELSH MELODY

All things bright and beautiful,
All creatures great and small,
All things wise and wonderful,
The Lord God made them all.
He gave us eyes to see them,
And lips that we might tell,
How great is God Almighty,
Who has made all things well.

—WILLIAM HENRY MONK

May the Lord bless you and keep you safe.
May the Lord make his face shine upon you,
and grant you grace.
May the Lord lift up His face unto you,
and give you peace,
now and forever more.

—*"Priestly blessing," Numbers 6:24–26*

This is full.
That is full.
From fullness, comes fullness.
When fullness is taken from fullness,
Fullness remains.
OM *shanti, shanti, shanti!*

—*Invocation from the Isha Upanishad*

Whichever God you worship,
I will answer your prayers.
Whatever path you take,
I will welcome you.

—*Bhagavad Gita 4:11*

Prayers of
Gratitude

Gratitude is much more than a way of praying; it is a way of being. And truly there is no better way to *be*. Choosing the lens of gratitude to look both outward and within, finding daily opportunities to give and receive appreciation, to experience what you have—rather than the anguish of what you don't have—your life will be unutterably blessed. What you see or perceive, and the emotions that accompany your "seeing," will literally change for the better. A powerful teaching attributed to the Torah reminds us: "You do not see the world as it is. You see the world as you are."

There's so much truth in that, and also in a similar teaching from Luke's gospel, 6:45: "The mouth gives voice to what fills the heart."

Letting gratitude fill your heart, seeing *deeply, living* the sacred, you will find more and more for which you can be grateful. You will waste less of your precious life and time on trivial complaints or heated outrage that life is not going exactly as it "should." And because you feel full (and supported) within yourself, you will be far less disturbed when things do go wrong or cause you grief or pain.

With gratitude as the chosen foundation of your life, you will grow more trusting and content. You will discover firsthand that suffering *is* part of life, but so are laughter, kindness, forgiveness, curiosity, awe, beauty and the rewards of love.

Gratitude's benefits extend, too, way beyond our individual existence. A grateful person is a gift to others. Accepting Love's invitation to contribute to a more compassionate and cooperative world, we become less demanding, more peaceful and far more inwardly poised. We find life more rewarding as well as more interesting, and complain far less. With that comes new levels of self-acceptance and self-appreciation that focus less on external achievement (as desired as that may be) than on the intrinsic meaning that life—and prayer—is continuously revealing to us, if only we can open ourselves to see it.

Prayers of gratitude make sacred the food we eat, the earth we share, the companionship and support of loved ones, and the efforts innumerable unknown people make on our behalf. They also make sacred whatever precious opportunities we have to appreciate and support other people. They make sacred what we learn from hard times, from "mistakes," from grief and the questions we can barely frame on the darkest of nights. There is holiness there, too. Always.

The familiarity and simplicity of some of these prayers and blessings should not distract you from their profound efficacy. Gratitude returns itself to us as trust, positivity and stability: priceless gifts to draw on in difficult times; equally priceless to offer in all the many moments when—with eyes open or closed—we simply murmur, "Thank you."

If your only prayer was thank you,
it would be enough.

—*Meister Eckhart*

My God, I give You this day.
I offer You, now, all the good I will do.
I promise to accept, for love of you,
all the difficulties I may meet.

Help me to make choices
through this day
in a manner that accords
with your highest desires for me.
Amen.

—*Adapted from a prayer attributed to Francis de Sales*

Whatever comes or may be,
no matter how light or dark,
I welcome you.
I do not weary.
For I know—
that the secret is the Lord's love.

Though all my friends will turn to dust,
and all my hopes will fade with the sun,
I welcome you.
I do not weary.
For I know—
that the secret is the Lord's love.

Whatever sadness or sorrow will come to me
I welcome you.
I do not weary.
For I know—
that the secret is the Lord's love.

Whatever joy sets my heart ablaze,
I welcome you.
Your coming and going
do not weary me.
For I know—
what my heart has always known,
that the secret is the Lord's love.

And when the final notes are played,
my plans turn to illusion,
and I smell the cosmic fire,
I will welcome you, my friend.

For I only know—
what I have always known,
that the secret is the Lord's love.

—KIM CUNIO

Divine Mother,
give me Your eyes so I can see myself through them
and see how holy in Your eyes is my soul,
and how holy in Your eyes is my mind,
and how holy in Your eyes is my heart,
and how holy and sacred in Your eyes is my body.
Help me be as merciful and generous with myself
as You would want me to be;

help me honor myself as I have found to my amazement
You honor me;
help me live and work from the peace and balance and compassion
from which You live and work and help.
Help me in these ways, Mother, so I can at last
truly become the instrument
You need me to become,
the sacred instrument of Your compassion in action
that you created me to be,
and that I already am in Your Holy and illumined eyes.

—ANDREW HARVEY

The Lord wishes it that our prayer and our trust be *large*!
We must know unreservedly that our Lord is the ground
from which our prayer grows.
This is a gift given in love.

God wants us to understand that we are
more truly in heaven than on earth . . .
We are of God.
That *is* what we are . . .
God did not have to begin to love us
because from the beginning
we have always been known and loved . . .
Gratitude appreciates who we really are.
Our thanking is to enjoy God!

—LADY JULIAN OF NORWICH

Does any prayer mean more than *Thank you*?

For this gift of life, *Thank you*.
For health and understanding, *Thank you*.
For patience, tolerance and forgiveness, *Thank you*.
For family, friends, and the kindness of strangers, *Thank you*.
For all the ways I am the same as others
and all the ways in which I am different, *Thank you*.
For what I learn as I fall down,
and what I learn rising up again, *Thank you*.
For the air I breathe, the water I drink, *Thank you*.
For the feet that carry me, *Thank you*.
For the ears with which I hear,
for the eyes with which I see, *Thank you*.
For arms that can reach out and hands that can touch, *Thank you*.
For knowing right from wrong, *Thank you*.
For living lovingly, *Thank you*.
For chances to be playful, fresh, creative, *Thank you*.
For chances to feel wonder, awe, delight, *Thank you*.
For chances to face sorrow and to comfort sorrow in others' lives,
Thank you.
For these words to pray, *Thank you*.
For all that prayer brings to me, *Thank you*.
For the sacred that is everywhere,
and where I am, Thank you.

—*S.D.*

Just as life exists within the smallest seed,
so the Beloved is in me.
And so the Beloved is in you.

Oh seekers, move past your arrogant assumptions.
Find the One that's in your own self.

You want the truth?
Let me tell you the truth.
Listen to the secret sound,
the real sound.
It's inside you.

—*KABIR*

I am praying again, Awesome One.
You hear me again, even while words
rising from those deepest, most inner places
rush toward you in the wind.

I yearn to be held
in the great hands of your heart.
Oh, let them take me now.
Into them I place these fragments: my life.
And you, God: spend them however you wish.

—*RAINER MARIA RILKE*

O Father, Mother, near unto every heart,
we fly to you,
seeking to feel your presence,
and, conscious of you,
to know you as you are
and to worship you
with our entire mind, conscience, heart and soul.

We seek to be at one with you for a moment,
to refresh hearts tired with the world's journey and with sore travel,
and to bow our faces down
and drink again at the living waters of your life.

O Infinite One,
we reverence you,
you who are the unchangeable in things that change,
the foundation of all that endures,
the loveliness of things beautiful,
the wisdom, justice and love
which make and hold and bless this world
of matter and people.

Before we call, you know our needs.
You do more for us than we could ask for, or imagine.

We know that you are our Father and our Mother,
that you fold in your arms all the worlds that you have made,
and warm, with a mother's breath, each mote of the sun's beams,
and that you bless each wandering, foolish child.

How marvellous your loving kindness is!
In loving kindness you made everything
and in tender mercy you watch over the world's troubles,
blessing those who sorrow,
calling back those who stray.

When our own hearts cry against us,
you, far greater than our heart,
still take us up,
bear us up on your wings,
and bless us with your infinite love.

—*Adapted from Theodore Parker*

Lord, this heart of mine is your temple.
These actions of mine are your handmaidens.
This body of mine is your home.
My senses testify to you.
My sleep rests in you.
My feet walk your journey.
My words are prayers.
Oh Lord, all that I say and
all that I do,
is worship.

—*Shankara*

It's not wearing holy robes or
speaking holy words
that liberates you.
It's bringing those words to life.

Craving nothing,
doing good,
this is a life of holiness.

—*The Dhammapada 1:9–10*

More, more, more?
Today I want to say: *enough, enough, enough.*
Sufficient unto the day!
Oh, and thanks be.

—*S.D.*

Having found, in many books,
different methods of going to God,
and diverse practices of spiritual life,
I thought this would serve rather to puzzle me
than to facilitate what I sought after, which was nothing
but how to become wholly God's . . .
I renounced for the love of Him everything that was not He;
and I began to live as though there was none but He and I
in the world . . .
I worshipped him the oftenest that I could,
keeping my mind in his Holy Presence,
and recalling it as often as I found it wandered from Him.
I found no small pain in this exercise,
and yet I continued it notwithstanding . . .
It begets holy freedom, and if I may so speak,
a familiarity with God wherewith we ask . . .
the graces we stand in need of.

—BROTHER LAWRENCE

A promise given to Hildegard (and all of us) in a vision:

I, God, am in your midst.
Whoever knows me will never fail.
Not in the heights.
Not in the depths.
Not in the breadths.
For I am Love,
which even the deepest ignorance
could never still.

—HILDEGARD OF BINGEN

Breathe on me, Breath of God,
Fill me with life anew;
That I may love what You do love,
And do what You would do.

Breathe on me, Breath of God,
Until my heart is pure;
Until my will is one with Yours,
To do and to endure.

Breathe on me, Breath of God,
Till I am wholly Thine;
Until this earthly part of me
Glows with your fire divine.

Breathe on me, Breath of God,
So shall I never die,
But live with You the perfect life,
Of your eternity.

—*ADAPTED FROM EDWIN HATCH*

The spirit of the valley is eternal.
This is called the mysterious female.
The gateway of the mysterious female
is called the source of heaven and earth.
Barely discernible, she hints at existence.
Yet when evoked,
her power is inexhaustible.

—*TAO TE CHING, VS. 6*

Rejoice in the Lord always.
And again I say, Rejoice!
Let your richness of spirit be known to all.
The Lord is at hand.
Let no anxiety make its home in your hearts,
but whatever your needs may be, by prayer and supplication,
and with thanksgiving,
let them be made known to God.
And the peace of God,
which exceeds anything that the mind can comprehend,
will protect your hearts and minds in the Being of Christ.
And finally, sisters and brothers,
whatever is true,
whatever is worthy of reverence,
whatever is good and holy,
whatever is lovely to look at and beautiful to hear,
everything that has virtue,
and everything that deserves praise,
let this be what fills your thinking . . .
And the God of peace will be with you.

—*Philippians 4:8–9*

Lead us from the unreal to the Real!
Lead us from darkness to light!
Lead us from death to immortality!
OM shanti, shanti, shanti.

—*Brihadaranyaka Upanishad 1:3:27*

I ask all blessings,
I ask them with reverence
of my mother—the earth,
of the sky, moon, and sun—my father.

I am old age: the essence of life,
I am the source of all happiness.
All is peaceful,
all in beauty,
all in harmony,
all in joy.

—*Attributed to the Navaho tradition,*
19th–20th centuries

Those who see God
in and through every action,
see God.

Better than any religious ritual
is the worship offered by wise actions.
Wisdom should be revealed in
all you do, Arjuna.

Wisdom is the boat that can carry you
across the tides of ignorance.

—*Bhagavad Gita 4:24, 33, 36*

There can be no water without the sea.
There can be no touch without skin.
There can be no smell without nose.
There can be no form without the eye.
There can be no sound without the ear.
There can be no wisdom without the heart.
There can be no work without hands.
There can be no walking without feet.
There can be no scriptures without the word.
There can be nothing without the Self.

—*Brihadaranyaka Upanishad 4:11*

You needn't leave your room.
Just sit at your table and listen.
You needn't even listen. Just wait.
You needn't even wait.
Just learn stillness.
Be still, alone with your own self.
The world will willingly give itself to you to be unmasked.
It has no choice.
It will writhe in bliss at your feet.

—*Franz Kafka*

God be in my head, and in my understanding.
God be in my eyes, and in my looking.
God be in my mouth, and in my speaking.
God be in my heart, and in my thinking.
God be in my end, and at my parting.

—*From the Sarum Primer*

These are the words of Christ:
"Call no man master, for ye all are brothers."
. . . It is almost another way of saying
that we must and will find Christ
in each and every man,
when we look on them as brothers [and sisters].

—DOROTHY DAY

I feel that a human being may be happy in this world and I know
that this world is a world of imagination and vision . . .

Everybody does not see alike.
To the eye of a miser, a guinea is far more beautiful than the sun.
And a bag worn with the use of money has more
beautiful proportions than
a vine filled with grapes.
The tree which moves some to tears of joy
is in the eyes of others only
a green thing which stands in the way.
As a man is, so he sees.
When the sun rises,
do you not see a round disk of fire
something like a gold piece?
O no, no, I see an innumerable company of
the Heavenly host crying,
"Holy, Holy, Holy is the Lord God Almighty."

I do not question my bodily eye any more than
I would question a window concerning sight.
I look through it and not with it.

—WILLIAM BLAKE

If it's God that you want to come close to, then
look for the Divine in the hearts of everyone you meet.
Speak well of them all.
Do this whether they are absent or present.
And if you want to be an example to other people,
then—just like the sun—you must show the same light to all.

To bring joy to one single heart
is far better than building many shrines for worship.

To enslave one soul with kindness
is far better than setting free a thousand slaves.

The true seeker sits in the middle of a crowd,
gets up in the morning,
eats, sleeps, marries, buys, sells,
gives and takes in the markets of life,
yet never forgets God for a single moment.

—*ABU SA'ID ABUL-KHAYR*

Father in heaven!
When thoughts of you stir in our hearts
let us not react like a frightened bird
seeking escape,
but like a child waking from sleep
with the smile of an angel.

—*SØREN KIERKEGAARD*

Heavenly Father, I thank you.
You have heard me.
I know that you hear me always.
I called out to you for the sake of those
who stand nearby—
that they can believe
you sent me.

—WORDS OF JESUS, JOHN 11:41–42

Blessed is the grace that crowns the sky with stars
and keeps the planets on their ways,
the law that turns night to day
and fills our eyes with light,
the love that keeps us whole
and day by day sustains us.

Praised be the Power
that brings renewal to the soul,
the vital song that makes the whole of creation dance.

Blessed is the murmuring dark
and blessed is light to the eyes.
The fall of dusk,
the turning of the day,
we give thanks for life's renewal,
the radiant return of the sun,
the blessed power of creation.
Praised be the light.

—TRADITIONAL JEWISH PRAYER AT YOM KIPPUR

Give what you are most eager to receive.
No gift is greater than a loving presence.

—*S.D.*

If it's freedom that drives your thinking,
happiness will bubble up within you.
Along with happiness, will come deep contentment.
When your mind is content, your body is peaceful.
When your body is peaceful, you will open to bliss.

It's happiness that will allow you to be in the present moment.
In the present moment, you can be mindful.
This means, you will see things as they really are.

Seeing life mindfully, you will perceive that life itself is a miracle.
Seeing that, you won't need to run after distractions.
And as your mind stops grasping for distractions,
you will know what it is to be free.

—*From the Digha Nikaya*

God came to my house and asked for charity.
I fell on my knees and cried, "Beloved, what may I give"?
"Just love," He said. "Just love."

—*Francis of Assisi*

Our Father who art in heaven,
hallowed be thy name.
Thy kingdom come,
Thy will be done on earth,
as it is in heaven.
Give us this day our daily bread,
and forgive us our trespasses,
as we forgive those who trespass against us.
And lead us not into temptation,
but deliver us from evil.

—*Matthew 6:9–13*

Hail Mary, full of grace,
Our Lord is with thee.
Blessed art thou among women,
and blessed is the fruit of thy womb,
Jesus.
Holy Mary, Mother of God,
pray for us now,
and at the hour of our death.

Glory be to the Father,
and to the Son,
and to the Holy Spirit,
as it was in the beginning is now,
and ever shall be,
world without end.
Amen.

—*Prayers of the traditional Catholic rosary*

Let us open our minds and hearts to all that we are.
And to all that we are becoming.
Each of us is a unique and irreplaceable being.
Each of us has strengths with which we are familiar,
and strengths that we have barely tapped.
Let us take a moment to remember our strengths,
and our gratitude for them.

Whatever imperfections we may believe our lives have,
our gift of life is utterly precious.
Let us take a moment to remember the uniqueness of our own lives.

Let us take a moment to value the sacredness of all lives:
the lives of the people we know;
the lives of the people we don't know.
Let us think about all other living forms,
and our interdependence with them.

Let us think about our gifts of gratitude,
appreciation, encouragement, kindness.
Let us remember how possible it is
to transform difficult situations
through the power of compassion.

Let us cultivate a hopeful and loving frame of mind,
in which compassion can grow.

Let us nourish and express our highest intentions.
Let our highest intentions come to life
through our actions.

May our prayers be of benefit to our entire human family.
May all beings live in happiness and peace.

—S.D.

PRAYERS IN
TIMES OF NEED
OR SORROW

If your prayer life begins—or begins again—at a time of intense need or sorrow, or at a time of death, you will be far from alone. This is true for many of us. Rather than worrying about whether your motives are worthy, simply be glad that you are now praying, however awkward or inexpert your prayers may initially feel. And never be afraid to bring to prayer, to God, your deepest needs or hurts, even your deepest shame.

Praying with a naked heart, perhaps with a heart that feels hurt or broken, you give yourself a perfect chance to experience how unconditional the path of love is, and how unstinting your welcome is on that path.

The prayers we choose or return to when we are most vulnerable are likely to penetrate very deeply into our being. I would urge you at such times to let your mind and feelings "rest" on a particular prayer. You might choose it instinctively, then read it through a few times. Perhaps you will find a single phrase that seems particularly comforting. Having done that, and perhaps after writing out the prayer in your own journal, let that special phrase be a mantra for you, steadying you as you repeat it, remembering that most of the prayers in this collection have served people just like you for centuries. In some cases, they have mended hearts and lives over millennia.

There are phrases in many of these prayers that have seen me through my own darkest and most self-doubting times. Truly, I can scarcely imagine how I would be here today, writing with such hope and heart, had those prayers and fragments of prayer not poured into my life.

With invitation as your only effort, you can let their renewal pour into your life.

Approach these prayers, and your intentions, gently. Make few demands on the prayers and fewer demands still on yourself. Let the depth of your need be met by the depth of these prayers. There is such beauty in these pages. Let the words soothe you, sing to you, comfort you just as a Divine Mother would. These are prayers and brief, essential teachings that have lifted me when I believed it would be impossible. They can lift you also.

Nothing whatsoever is higher than I, Arjuna.
All worlds, all beings are strung upon me
like jewels on a single string.

I am the taste in the water.
I am the light in the moon and the sun.
Mine is the sacred sound *OM,*
and the hush in the air.

I am the humanness in people.
I am the fragrance of the earth.
I am the brilliance that is in fire.
And the life in those who live . . .

Know me as the eternal seed in all of existence.
as the wisdom of the wise,
as the splendour of the splendid,
as the strength of the strong . . .

All states of being begin in me.
They are *in* me, not I in them . . .

I am with all beings always;
I abandon no one.
However great your sorrows,
you are never separated from me.

—*Bhagavad Gita 7:7–12, 9:32*

Father and Mother of All that I AM,
may I be fully present in this time and this place.
May I accept myself just the way I am.
May I accept my brothers and sisters just the way they are.
May I accept life as it is unfolding right now.

May I take All that Is into my heart
and be at peace with it.
May All that Is be at peace with me.
May I give and receive that blessing.
May I dwell in that communion.

May I surrender my little will to your great Will
which holds all beings in perfect equality.
May I surrender the conditions I place on love
that I may give love and receive love
without conditions.

May my heart open,
releasing fear and desire.
May my mind open,
releasing judgments and interpretations.
May my life open,
releasing expectations,
so that I may embrace what is
and see it truly.

May my openness invite your presence.
May my surrender inspire your grace.
Amen.

—*Paul Ferrini*

The noblest prayer is when
those who pray
are inwardly transformed
into what they kneel
and bow before.

—*Angelus Silesius*

A new heart I will give you.
And a new spirit I will put within you.
And I will take out of your flesh
the heart of stone;
And give you a heart of flesh.
And I will put my spirit within you,
and cause you to walk in my ways.

—*Ezekiel 36:26–27*

Peace and universal love is the essence of the gospel
preached by all who are enlightened.
The Lord has preached that equanimity is the way.
Forgive do I creatures all, and let all creatures forgive me.
Unto all do I extend the hand of friendship.
Unto none do I feel enmity.
Be clear that violence is the root cause of all
the miseries in the world.
Violence enslaves those who are gripped by it.
"Do not injure any living being."

This is the eternal, perennial, and unalterable law of
spiritual life.
No weapon is greater than non-violence and love.

—A TEACHING FROM THE JAINS,
A TRADITION OF TOTAL NON-VIOLENCE

Here's what we know:
human beings thrive in the presence of love.
We grow more loving where love is present.
. . . We receive love more confidently when we feel able to give it.
We feel more alive when breathing in love
and breathing out love
become, simply, breathing.

—S.D. IN SEEKING THE SACRED

Once you get a clear idea of what life's about,
you don't have to talk too much about it.
Just live it in your own way.
When we aren't forcing our ideas on other people,
life's rewards come more easily to us.

The perfume of flowers fades quickly.
The ripeness of fruit is over in days.
Our time in this life is short.
Don't leave yourself with the possibility of regret.
Take every chance to love life in its mysterious depths.

In difficult moments, remember that everything passes.
Sit quietly inside your home.
Remind yourself that spring will come again.

—LOY CHING YUEN

When you know beyond any doubting
that a single life force
flows through everything,
and that *you are this life*,
then you will love all beings
naturally and effortlessly.

And when you realise the depth and fullness
of love for your own self,
you will know that every living being
and the entire universe
are included in your care.

You are not *in* the body.
The body is in you.

—TRADITIONAL VEDANTA TEACHING

Heavenly Father,
please increase in me at this time
your life-giving power.

—AGNES SANFORD

I know there is but One Mind,
which is the Mind of God,
in which all people live and move
and have their being.

—ERNEST HOLMES

Unless you become as little children,
you will not enter the kingdom of heaven.

—WORDS OF JESUS, MATTHEW 18:3

I can appreciate and love life wholeheartedly
and in the present moment.
I can experience life now and forever
as holy and infinitely precious.
Whatever my age, whatever my circumstances,
I can reignite in my own life a child's passion and love for humanity,
a child's curiosity, awe, sweet tenderness and joy.
I can learn from the world's children.
I can learn from the child I once was.
I can bless the world with what I find.

—S.D.

Sometimes
when people sit on their cushions to meditate,
they feel isolated.
But they are not isolated.

We all share the same air.
We share this ground.
We share food, water, everything.
We are all sharing,
and we are all interconnected,
not just with ordinary sentient beings,
but also with many, many layers of
higher evolved beings.
They are all here to support us.

—*JETSUNMA TENZIN PALMO*

With a branch which was never like that one,
God the tree will eventually come, announcing
summer and murmuring with ripeness.
In a land where people lean closer to hear,
where everyone is just as lonely as I.

For this will be revealed only to the solitary,
and even more will be given to many others
who share this solitude than to the poor one.
For to each a different God appears
until they recognize, close to tears,
that through their wide-open pondering,
through all their knowing and negating,
differing only among His hundreds,
One God wanders like a wave.

This is the most definitive prayer
that those keeping watch declare:
God the root has borne fruit;
go forth and shatter the bells.

We come to the quieter days
in which the hour stands ripe;
God the root has borne fruit:
be earnest and watch.

—RAINER MARIA RILKE
(TRANSLATED BY MARK S. BURROWS)

Bless me, that I can clearly see my
unconditional reliance upon others,
and can think about them with a concern as great
as the concern I have for myself.
A buddha works only for others.
An immature person works only for himself.

Worrying only about your own welfare
brings grief.
Joy comes when we begin to grow conscious
that all beings have served us like mothers
through countless lifetimes.

Seeing the value of my life reflected
in the lives of all others,
I am rescued from selfishness.

—MAHAYANA BUDDHIST TEACHING

Our path is not to judge, but to heal:
to create the circumstances
where healing can begin.

—FROM A COURSE IN MIRACLES

Beloved: as I face this latest challenge,
I am aware how unclear I feel.
I open my heart to your clarity,
to your knowing,
to guide my choices.

May I be trusting enough,
may I be still enough,
to hear and heed the wisdom that is within me.

Thank you for the presence of Love.
It is with me at this time and always.

—HILARY STAR

Get over your hesitations!
Don't dwell on disappointments.
Delight in your life.
Be an example to those who need it.
Reveal the path to many.

—ADAPTED FROM THE SUTTA NIPATA

Arranging a bowl of flowers in the morning
can give a sense of quiet in a crowded day—
like writing a poem,
or saying a prayer.
What matters is that one be, for a time,
inwardly attentive.

—ANNE MORROW LINDBERGH, IN A GIFT FROM THE SEA

Love those with whom you share this world.
Where love is present, no one is harmed.
Love fulfills God's longing for the world.
We know the urgent mystery of this time.
The hour has come to wake from sleep.
Insight calls.
Night is over; day is near.
Lay aside whatever lingers in the shadows.
Dress yourself in the robes of light.
Live honorably.

In celebration of this day,
let your life be worthy of its light.

—*Romans 13:9–12*

The power to make positive choices is the greatest gift
we human beings have.
Whatever your outward circumstances,
it allows you to be the author of your own life . . .
free to ask "Is this loving?"

—*S.D., in The Universal Heart*

Dear children, let us not love with words or tongue alone
but with actions and in truth.

The mouth gives voice to what fills the heart.

—*Luke 6:45; 1 John 3:18*

Know with unwavering certainty that all spiritual
ideals are expressions of the same supreme Presence.
Blessed is the soul who has known that all is one.

—RAMAKRISHNA

To develop compassion for others,
you must discover compassion for yourself.
To have compassion for yourself,
you must understand what you share with others.
Often what causes us to be most defensive, angry or critical
has deep roots in our own emotional history.
Yet what you most want to avoid or condemn,
may be your most essential teacher.
Understanding your interconnections with others,
and that your suffering is echoed in others' lives,
you heal your world—and your own dear heart.

Breathing in and breathing out,
I offer myself the gifts of unconditional acceptance;
unconditional appreciation;
unconditional forgiveness;
unconditional loving-kindness.

Accepting all of who I am,
I offer acceptance and compassion to others.
I breathe in compassion for myself,
and breathe out compassion for all beings.

[Repeating these two short, profound verses may be enough for many weeks or months. If it is enough, please stop here.]

Breathing in and breathing out,
I offer to all beings, known and unknown,
the gifts of unconditional acceptance;
unconditional appreciation;
unconditional forgiveness;
unconditional loving-kindness.
I send love without reservation to wherever it is needed.
I am part of the world's suffering.
I am part of the world's healing.

Keeping myself safe,
and seeing myself as a source of safety for others,
I vow to live peacefully.
I wish no one harm.
I wish healing for all.
I welcome peace for all.
I vow to live peacefully.
I offer to others the peace that lives in my own
life and heart.
Blessed be.

—S.D.

God does not despise what He has made.
For love of our souls, made in His likeness,
God does not hesitate to be with us in our
simple bodily needs.

In the same way that the body is clothed in cloth,
and the muscles are held within skin,
and the bones within muscles,
and the heart within our chest,
so are we,
body and soul,
held in the goodness of God.

Yes! And even more intimately—
because all these vanish and waste away
but the goodness of God
is constant and constantly near;
beyond comparing.

—*LADY JULIAN OF NORWICH*

Just as a river has its source
in a far-off spring,
so the human life
has its source also.
To find that source,
is to uncover the secret
of heaven and earth.

—*LAO-TZU*

O Lord, make haste
to help me.

—*PSALM 70:1*

A single candle,
lit in my heart or hand,
restores hope.

Beloved Spirit:
Help us to see ourselves as you do.
Help us to see how hope connects us
to the deepest wellsprings of our existence,
and to all that is most sacred.

Beloved Spirit:
let us call on hope each day of our lives.
Let us live hopefully.
Let us recognize each new moment of possibility,
and welcome it bravely.

Beloved Spirit:
Help us to remember that darkness and despair will pass.
Help us to remember that dawn will come again.
In the knowledge of love, we are reborn.
Blessed be.

—*S.D.*

Make every thought an offering to me.
Meditate upon me constantly.

Using these deepest gifts,
and through my grace,
you will overcome all difficulties.

—*Bhagavad Gita 8:7, 14*

The One who is invited is inside you and is inside me.
We all know the plant lives deep within the seed.
Each one of us is trying to emerge. None of us has gone far.
Let any false pride fall away.
Look around inside.
The blue sky opens out toward infinity.
That familiar sense of "not enough" falls away.
The harm I've caused myself becomes unimportant.
Infinite suns emerge
whenever I place myself confidently in that inner world.
Kabir speaks: Student, tell me, what is God?
The breath that breathes inside breath.

—*KABIR*

Returning to simplicity,
your desires are tamed.
When your desires are tamed,
you discover stillness.
In stillness, the world is made new.

—*LAO-TZU*

The world's rivers empty themselves into the Great Ocean,
which, though entirely full, receives them undisturbed.
In the same way you can witness
the flow of needs and desires in your own mind
without disturbance:
neither condemning them nor running after them.
This is what peace is.

—*BHAGAVAD GITA 2:70–71*

I am now free from fear, anxiety,
worry, dread, and suspense.
I have faith in Thy Holy Spirit,
and I trust Thee to protect me,
to provide for me,
and to bring all my affairs into divine order.

—CHARLES AND CORA FILLMORE

Don't let anything make you anxious.
Don't let anything frighten you.
Everything passes.
Only God is unchanging.

—TERESA OF AVILA

Between me and You, there is only me.
Take away the me, and only You remain.

—MANSUR AL-HALLAJ

Mirabai says: "The passion of your midnight tears
is bringing you to God."

—MIRABAI

Help me, God.
Help me.
Help me not to understand
but to know:
to know that You are with me,
to know that my loved ones are Your loved ones also,
to know that I can bear the impossible,
to know that suffering fades,
to know that help comes in unexpected guises,
to know that Life in all its fullness is always present,
to know that compassion arises when we call for it,
to know that help comes.
Help me, God.

—S.D.

One day I stopped in front of a Cézanne still-life—
green apples, a white plate and a cloth.
Being tired, restless,
and distracted by the stream of bored Sunday afternoon sightseers
drifting through the galleries,
I simply sat and looked,
too inert to remember whether I ought to like it or not.
Slowly I became aware that something was pulling me out of my
vacant stare and the colors were coming alive, gripping
my gaze till I was soaking myself in their vitality.
Gradually a great delight filled me . . .
It had all happened by just sitting still and waiting.

—JOANNA FIELD, IN A LIFE OF ONE'S OWN

A Meditation on Wisdom

Wisdom is an expression of the One Self in whom we all live.
Wisdom is an expression of who I am.
Wisdom is a way of learning what I am.
Wisdom and humility grow side by side.
I can allow myself to be wise.
Whenever I stand at a crossroads,
I can choose the path of wisdom.

The message of Christ my teacher is plain.
Love one another as he loved us.
Love is the finest expression of wisdom.
Caring for others as I would wish to be cared for,
I discover wisdom.

Wisdom does no harm.
Wisdom seeks what is good.
Wisdom does not impose itself on others.
Wisdom can be light, joyous,
sensual and appreciative.
It can also be heavy with sorrow or shaded with regret.
Wisdom is kind.

I trust myself enough to know
that sometimes I will not be wise.
Let me learn from my mistakes,
so I will not need the same lesson again.

Trusting that wisdom comes from God,
I can accept that wisdom has its own timetable.
There are no simple answers to all questions.
There are no easy ways to understand all of life's mysteries.
Wisdom teaches me patience, without indifference.

Turning inward, let us pray: that we can fill this day with wisdom,
that we can fill this day with wisdom and love in full
measure. Turning outward, we ask that we can fill this day with
wisdom and love in full measure.
We ask this not only for ourselves but for all who live on this earth.
May we know happiness.
May we live in harmony with one another.
May we nourish wisdom.

—S.D.

If something can be done when trouble comes,
what reason is there to be downcast?
If nothing can be done,
what reason is there to be downcast?

—Shantideva

The peace we yearn for is already within . . .
Every human heart is already enfolded
in the capacity to feel peace
as the direct result of
loving-kindness, compassion,
and truthfulness.

—Paul R. Fleischman

O Lord, you have looked for me.
You know me.
You know when I sit down.
You know when I get up.

Even my thoughts are known to you.
Indeed, before I speak,
You know what I will say.
You surround my entire existence:
behind, in front.

Your hand is in mine.
It's almost too wonderful to think of this.
It's beyond my powers of comprehension.

Where could I escape you?
Where could I avoid your presence?
If I rise to heaven, there you are.
If I make my bed in Sheol, there you are.

If I go on the wings of dawn to the edges of the oceans,
even there your hand will lead me,
and your right hand will keep me safe.

Were I to say, "I can hide in the darkness,
as day becomes night," yet,
even darkness is not dark to you, O Lord.
To you, the darkest night is bright as the day.

PSALM 139:1–12

All that we should have thought, and didn't think,
All that we should have said, and didn't say,
All that we should have done and didn't do,
All that we ought not to have thought—and did think,
All that we ought not to have spoken—and did say,
All that we ought not to have done—and did do,
For thoughts, words, actions, we pray, O God,
for forgiveness.

—*Adapted from the Zend-Avesta*

May we hear only that which benefits all.
May we see only that which benefits all.
May we serve you, O Lord and Giver of Life!
May we be your instruments
to spread peace on this earth.
OM *shanti, shanti, shanti.*

—*Invocation from Prashna Upanishad*

Envisage a place of uninterrupted peace.
Let your mind and thoughts rest there.
When you feel ready,
visualize a spiritual teacher or guide sitting quietly beside you.
This could be Jesus or Mary,
your guardian angel,
a wise being, a Guru,
or the historical Buddha.

It could be someone who has shown you kindness.
Just be in that place together.
Draw on the energy of peace.
Take in its beauty. Let it heal your wounds.
Be aware of how it feels to have peace around you,
and rising within you.
Be aware of how it feels to sit with a being of deep,
unalterable peace.
Let yourself know: *I am not alone.*

I am a being of peace.
I embrace peace, compassion and kindness.
This is the foundation of my existence.
I am not alone.

—S.D.

Bring us, O Lord God, at our last awakening
into the house and gate of heaven,
to enter into that gate and dwell in that house,
where there shall be
no darkness nor dazzling, but one equal light;
no noise nor silence, but one equal music;
no fears nor hopes, but one equal possession;
no ends nor beginnings, but one equal eternity;
in the habitations of thy glory and dominion,
world without end.
Amen.

—JOHN DONNE

[At a time of death]
The body falls away.
We grieve its passing.
We miss its beauty, its familiarity and its utter preciousness.
Our hearts feel broken.
What does not fall is the soul, the spirit, the essential Oneness.
The spirit, that essence of each one of us, can only rise.
Rising is its very nature.

As it rises, *these* moments and *those* moments grow closer.
Even "here" and "there" loses meaning.
All one.

Only this finite life finishes.
Only this body.
In Oneness, there is no leaving.
There is no end.
Just unfolding.
Is it possible to remember the presence of our
loved one as a grace?

Grace comes in *through* the remembering. So does love.
Love is eternity's expression.
And love, we know, is never lost.

In love we come.
In love we return.
In love we remain.
Now. And forevermore.
Blessed be.

—*S.D.*

A deer craves fresh, running water.
In just that same way, my soul craves for you, O my God.
My soul thirsts for God, for the living God.
When will the time come for me to see the face of God?

—*Psalm 42:1–2*

My feet stand in a steady place.
Among the people of the world,
I will bless the Lord.

—*Psalm 26:12*

I will sing you, my God.
I will praise you.
I will bless your name throughout eternity.
Every day I will bless you.

Your goodness pours out to all.
Your tenderness is known in every land.

—*Psalm 145:1–3, 9*

No struggle is needed to reach God!
The only struggle called for
is to overcome whatever ignorance
keeps you from Him.

—ADAPTED FROM PARAMAHANSA YOGANANDA

This day, like any day, you may wake up empty and fearful.
Before you begin your day's efforts and thinking,
pick up an instrument and make music.

Let the beauty you most love be what you do.
There are countless ways to kneel and kiss the ground.

—RUMI

No coward soul is mine,
No trembler in the world's storm-troubled sphere:
I see Heaven's glories shine,
And faith shines equal, arming me from fear.

O God within my breast,
Almighty, ever-present Deity!
Life—that in me has rest,
As I—undying Life—have power in Thee!

Vain are the thousand creeds
That move men's hearts: unutterably vain;
Worthless as withered weeds,
Or idlest froth amid the boundless main,

To waken doubt in one
Holding so fast by Thine infinity;
So surely anchored on
The steadfast rock of immortality.

With wide-embracing love
Thy Spirit animates eternal years,
Pervades and broods above,
Changes, sustains, dissolves, creates and rears.

Though earth and man were gone,
And suns and universes cease to be,
And Thou wert left alone,
Every existence would exist in Thee.

There is not room for Death,
Nor atom that his might could render void;
Thou—Thou art Being and Breath,
And what Thou art may never be destroyed.

—*Last lines written by Emily Brontë*

Your body is mortal.
There's no escaping that.
You, though, are an immortal Self.
Your body is vulnerable to both pleasure and pain.
No one who identifies only with the body
can avoid this need for pleasure,
and fear of pain.
It is only when you realize that "you" is not your body,

that you become free.
Freedom brings you unceasing joy.

—CHANDOGYA UPANISHAD 12:1

You ask me why I entered the mountain deep and cold,
a place painful to climb and difficult to descend,
a place where the gods of the mountain live,
and the spirits of trees.
Have you not seen, O have you not seen,
the peach and plum blossoms in the royal garden?
Flying high and low, all over the garden petals scatter . . .

Have you not seen, O have you not seen,
that this has been our human fate?
Thinking of this, my heart feels torn . . .

I have never tired of watching the pine trees
and the rocks at Koyasan.

The clear stream of the mountain
brings unceasing joy.
Give up your pride in earthly glories.
Nothing will let us enter the eternal realms
but illumination in silence.

—KOBO DAISHI (KUKAI)

Lord, help me.
My boat is so small.
Your ocean is so immense.

—ADAPTED FROM A TRADITIONAL FRENCH MEDIEVAL PRAYER

Holy ones, angelic forces
when I have no answers, sustain me;
when I have no solutions, sustain me;
when I feel abandoned, sustain me;
when I feel no hope, sustain me;
when my hands remain empty, sustain me;
when I feel too small, sustain me;
when I know I am "not enough," sustain me;
when I am ashamed or shamed, sustain me;
when my sorrows overwhelm me, sustain me.
Open my heart and mind to a fresh vision of love.
Let love move through me and within me.
O bringers of Love: sustain me.

—S.D.

O Father,
Give the spirit power to climb
To the fountain of all light, and be purified.
Break through the mists of earth,
the weight of the clod, and
shine forth in splendor.
You are calm weather.
And quiet resting place for faithful souls.
To see You is the end, and the beginning.
You support us. You go before us.
You are the journey.
And journey's end.

—ADAPTED FROM BOETHIUS

Since duality does not exist, separation is not real.
Even "mind" is not a separate thing.
Unhindered, it shines forth for all beings.

Look inside your own mind.
Even though the clear light of reality
shines inside our own minds,
most of us seek this outside ourselves.

—PADMASAMBHAVA

My peace I leave with you.
My peace I give to you.
This is beyond the peace the world knows.
Do not let your hearts be troubled.
Do not be afraid.

—WORDS OF JESUS, JOHN 14:27

PRAYERS TO LIGHT
THE WAY

Prayer can be our most effective guide and teacher. Together with study and reflection, it is certainly that for me. It's comfort, too, and a re-experiencing of soul and spirit. "Lighting the way," prayer—and everything that prayer allows—literally shows us who and what we are. It draws us out from the shadows that fear or unworthiness can create. It shows us life as *good*, shows us our own lives as *good*, even when pain or sorrow is present.

A Course in Miracles teaches: "You are altogether irreplaceable in the Mind of God. No one else can fill your part of it. . . . To accept your littleness is arrogant, because it means that you believe your evaluation of yourself is truer than God's."

That is a truly startling teaching, and it may surprise you. Or you may wonder if it applies to you. Our habits of inadequacy can run deep and the idea of embracing life fully, much less claiming our sacred nature, is foreign to many of us. Yet why should it *not* be you who is a channel for divine grace, who is a unique expression of compassion, an embodiment of hope, kindness, forgiveness or good humor? Why should it *not* be you who is an instrument of love upon this earth?

Authentic spiritual leaders inevitably embody a humility, peace and stability of mind that can only emerge from prayer and meditation. Mahatma Gandhi exquisitely said: "My wisdom comes from the Highest Source . . . I bow to that wisdom in you." No matter how demanding his external schedule is, His Holiness the Dalai Lama spends hours every day in spiritual practices. Albert Schweitzer, Dom Bede Griffiths, Dr. Martin Luther King Jr., Thomas Merton and Dorothy Day all drew their most essential sustenance from daily hours of prayer.

Theirs may seem an impossibly high standard to follow and yet, without the knowledge of our inner world that prayer brings, you and I must rely on our ego rather than our soul strengths. That can make setbacks hard to bear. It makes us quick to judge others, sometimes with painful superficiality.

It's not by chance that the wisdom traditions call those who are truly compassionate *enlightened*. Literally, they have seen "the light" of life's meaning. They know what matters. They know what matters very little. And we can follow their example. Our efforts to live more generously, simply and peacefully; our evolving compassion for others; our vital protection of the physical world; everyday encounters that are cheerful, respectful, forgiving and kind: all of this is truly illuminated by and through prayer. Prayer shines a light and creates light. Prayer also brings the courage to express it.

There is a light that
shines beyond all things
on earth.
Beyond the highest,
oh, the very highest heavens.
This is the light that shines within your heart.

—*From the Chandogya Upanishad*

Inspirer of my mind,
consoler of my heart,
healer of my spirit:
Thy presence lifteth me from earth to heaven.
Thy words flow as the sacred river;
Thy thoughts riseth as a divine spring;
Thy tender feelings waken sympathy in my heart.
Beloved Teacher: Thy very being is forgiveness.
The clouds of doubt and fear are scattered by
Thy piercing glance;
all ignorance vanishes in Thy illuminating presence;
a new hope is born in my heart
by breathing Thy peaceful atmosphere.
O inspiring Guide through life's puzzling ways,
in Thee I feel abundance of blessing.

—*Hazrat Inayat Khan*

May we use our ears to hear what is good!
May we use our eyes to see what is fine!
May we serve you throughout our lives, Lord of Love!
May love and harmony be with us all.
OM shanti, shanti, shanti.

—I<small>NVOCATION FROM THE</small> P<small>RASHNA</small> U<small>PANISHAD</small>

In the world of the senses, change is constant.
The Lord of Love never changes.
Meditate on him.
Let your thoughts be absorbed in him.
Wake up from this illusion of a separate reality!

Recognize God.
Everything that limits you will fall away.
When you cease to identify with this temporary body
in which you live,
you will transcend simplistic ideas of birth and death.
Everything you desire will be satisfied.
Surrendering to the One who has no equal,
your yearning will be fulfilled.

—S<small>HVETASHVATARA</small> U<small>PANISHAD</small> 10, 11

You, O God, are our safe place
and our strength.
You help us constantly in times of trouble.
We have nothing to fear.

Even if the earth should change,
even if the mountains were to disappear into the sea

and the ocean's waters were to roar and foam,
there is an inner river, the streams of which make your city glad,
making us glad everywhere that you are known.

Nations may be in an uproar.
Kingdoms may collapse.
Yet at the sound of your voice the earth gentles.

You are with us, our silent center.
You may cause wars to cease . . . to cease forever.
You may break the bows and shatter the spears.
You may burn shields with fire.

Be still, and know that I am God.
Be still, and know.
Be still and know that I am what the people seek.
I am what the earth praises.

You are with us.

—PSALM 46

You are gods, all of you.
You are children of the Most High.
Nonetheless, you will die like all mortal creatures.
You will fall like any prince.

Rise up, O God!
Witness our earthly existence.
Every nation belongs to you.

—PSALM 82:6–8

Is it not written in your law that God said,
you are gods?
Why do you accuse me of blaspheming when I say
I am God's son?
If I am not doing what my Father wishes,
then ignore what I say.
But if I am carrying out my Father's wishes,
even if you don't believe in me,
believe what I do.
Believe, too, that I am in the Father,
and that the Father is in me.

—*Words of Jesus, John 10:34, 36, 37–38*

Love wisdom like a sister.
Regard insight like a cherished member
of your own family.

—*Proverbs 7:4*

Beloved: it's wisdom I need.
And trust to benefit from it.
I am trusting that
the strength and peace that flow from wisdom
are there for the asking.
I am trusting that
wisdom is less often found in the big gestures of our lives
than in the modest moments
unfolding as we live them.
I am trusting that
wisdom can be salvaged from the times
when I have failed utterly to be wise.

Wisdom, like grace,
like the air we breathe
and the water we drink,
and the earth we walk on,
and the inspiration we rely upon,
and the love we live for,
is your gift for your family.
Let me trust that.

—S.D.

Believe nothing because someone brilliant has said it.
Believe nothing because "everyone" believes it.
Believe nothing because it's been written down.
Believe nothing because someone says it's divine.
Believe nothing because someone else believes it.
Believe only what you yourself discover as true.

—TEACHING ATTRIBUTED TO THE BUDDHA

No matter how famous the mouth,
Check the word against experience.
We are here to do.
And through learning to know;
And through knowing to wonder;
And through wonder to attain simplicity;
And through simplicity to give attention;
and through attention
to see what needs to be done.

—FROM THE PIRKEI AVOT

God is neither plain meaning
nor just mystery.
God is meaning
that transcends mystery,
meaning that mystery alludes to,
meaning that speaks through mystery.

The meaning beyond mystery seeks
to come to expression.
The destiny of human being is
to articulate what is concealed.
The divine seeks to be disclosed
in the human.

—*Rabbi Abraham J. Heschel, in* Who Is Man?

Without going out of your door,
you can know the whole world.
Without looking out of your window,
you can discover the ways of heaven.

The further we travel,
the less we know.

Someone who's wise
gets there without travelling.
Sees, without looking.
Does, without doing.

—*Tao Te Ching, Vs. 47*

Jesus said:
I am the light that covers everything.
I am all.
From me all things have come.
Toward me, all things reach.
Split the wood. You will find me there.
Lift the stone. I am there.

—*Gospel of Thomas* 77

For as long as I am in the world,
I am the light of the world.

—*Words of Jesus, John 9:5*

I saw that there was an ocean of darkness and death
but I saw that there was an infinite ocean
of Light and Life and Love
that flowed over the ocean of darkness;
in that I *saw* the infinite Love of God.

—*George Fox*

The light of your body is your eye.
When your eye sees clearly,
your entire being is illuminated,
but if your eye is clouded,
then the life of your body will also be clouded.
Take care that the light within you isn't dimmed.
If your entire being is filled with light,
with no part of it left in the shadows,
there will be a shining radiance within you.
It will be as bright as if a lamp shines within you.

—*Words of Jesus, Luke 11:34–36*

Watch, dear Lord, with those
who wake or weep tonight.
Let your angels guard those who sleep.
Tend the sick.
Refresh the weary.
Comfort those who are dying.
Soothe the suffering.
Have mercy on those who are distressed.
We ask this for your love's sake.

—*Augustine of Hippo*

There's no way that I would want to suffer.
Yet what I most long for most urgently causes suffering.
How foolish I am!

—*Shantideva*

I have no bodily existence.
Universal kindness is my godly body.
I have no physical power.
Constancy is my strength.
I have no spiritual knowledge—
except that given to me by Wisdom.
I have no power—
except that of gentleness.

—ORACLE OF SUMIYOSHI

I am not the equal of the King.
I reflect the light He reveals through me.

—RUMI

There are three rungs on the ladder to God:
fear of God;
hope of divine reward;
friendship with God.

—GREGORY OF NYSSA

There are three spiritual states available to you.
In the first, you pay no attention to the sacred
and worship anything except God [sex, money, authority].
In the second, you discover something deeper,
and serve nothing and no one
other than God.

In the third, you are free to go beyond these divergences.
You neither claim to serve God nor not to serve God.
From those people, nothing disturbs the silence.

—*Rumi*

Rejoice in the Lord always.
Again I will say, rejoice.
Let your happiness be known to everyone.
The Lord is near.
Do not worry about anything,
but in everything by prayer and supplication
and with thanksgiving
let what you most need be made known to God.
And the peace of God, that soars beyond everyday thinking,
will protect your hearts and minds in Jesus Christ.

—*Philippians 4:4–7*

Let the peace of Christ
overflow in your hearts.
You have been called to unity.
Be thankful.

—*Colossians 3:15*

The kingdom of heaven
is spread upon the earth,
and humankind does not see it.

—*Gospel of Thomas, 113:16*

Open your eyes.
The whole world is filled with God.

—*Johann Wolfgang von Goethe*

Look through the Beloved's eyes.
It's the Beloved you will see.
Everywhere.

—*Rumi*

. . . All must love the human form,
In heathen, Turk, or Jew;
Where Mercy, Love, and Pity dwell
There God is dwelling too.

—*William Blake*

In Christ,
there is no longer Jew or Greek,
slave or master,
male or female.
You are all one,
in Christ Jesus.

—*Galatians 3:28*

United in bliss,
there is neither father nor mother,
gods, or sacred teachings.
There is neither thief nor slayer,
neither low caste nor high,
monk nor ascetic.
The Self is beyond good and evil,
is beyond any suffering of the human heart.

United in bliss,
one sees without seeing,
smells without smelling,
tastes without tasting,
speaks without speaking,
hears without hearing,
touches without touching,
thinks without thinking,
knows without knowing,
for there is nothing separate from him.
O, there is nothing separate from him.

Where there is unity in life,
one without a second one,
this is the world of Brahman,
this is the ultimate goal in life,
the ultimate treasure,
the supreme joy.
Those who fail to seek this goal,
experience only a shadow of this joy.

—FROM THE BRIHADARANYAKA UPANISHAD

The seed of God is in us.
Given an intelligent farmer and a faithful field hand,
it will thrive and grow up to God
whose seed it is and, accordingly,
its fruit will be God-nature.
Pear seeds grow into pear trees.
Nut seeds grow into nut trees.
God-seeds into God.

Go to the depths of the soul,
the secret place of the Most High,
to the roots,
to the heights.
For everything that God can do,
is there.

—*Meister Eckhart*

Whatever is vulnerable to change isn't your real life.
Within each of us is another body. Another beauty.
Its source is the Light that never changes.

What we must do is discover how to mingle with this Light:
how to become one with what's Unchanging.
What we must do is realize and understand this truth.

This is why we are in the world.
Within your heart is a space smaller even than an atom.
There, God has placed the 18,000 universes.

—*Bawa Muhaiyaddeen*

It's no small matter for a soul given to restless thoughts
to realize the truth:
that God is within you.
And to understand that you don't need
to go to heaven in order to speak to the eternal Father—
or enjoy His company . . .

Nor do you need wings to find Him.
You only need stillness, and a willingness to look within.
No need either to let confusion overcome you
before such a merciful Guest.
Rather, with utter humility,
talk to Him as you would to a beloved Father:
ask for what you want;
tell your sorrows;
seek to be free.

—*Adapted from Teresa of Avila*

The wise, through sitting quietly in meditation,
recognize the Self.
Hidden in the cave of the heart,
they can leave behind both pleasure and pain.
Those who know they are neither body nor mind,
but the eternal Self,
the divine principle of existence,
find the source of happiness
and live in happiness.
I see the gates of happiness opening for you.

Hidden in every heart
is the Self.

Smaller than smallest,
greater than greatest.
Sorrow has no claim on those
who subdue their demands
and bathe in the glory of the One,
the Self,
through the grace of the Lord of Love.

—*Katha Upanishad 1:12,13, 20*

The Tao is close, but you look far away.
Life is simple. Yet you look for problems.

—*Taoist philosophy, c. 200 BC*

Fill your bowl to the brim and it will spill.
Keep sharpening your knife and it will blunt.
Chase after money and fame and your body will tense.

Worry too much about what other people are thinking,
and you will be their prisoner.

Do what is right.
Then step back.
This is the path to peacefulness.

—*Tao Te Ching, Vs. 9*

The first sign of your becoming religious is that you are
becoming cheerful.
When someone is gloomy, his condition may be dyspepsia,
but it is not religion.
To the yogi, everything is bliss.
Every human face that he sees brings cheerfulness to him.

—SWAMI VIVEKANANDA

The language of God is silence.
Yet signs can also speak.
A smile here, a word there,
a plant that's survived drought or frost,
a phone call that ends an awkward silence,
someone else's needs to be answered or met.
The cat that doesn't judge your pajamas or achievements.
The child who takes your hand.
The friend who's safe enough to weep or laugh.
Your own willingness to die and rise again.

—S.D.

O God, whatever you would grant me in this life,
Give it to my enemies.
O God, whatever you would give me in the life to come,
Give it to my friends.
You are enough for me.
O God, if I worship you because I fear hell,
then burn me repeatedly.

And if I worship you
only to get to heaven,
then close its gate in my face.
But if I worship you for your own sake,
Then reveal to me your eternal beauty.

—*RABI'A AL-BASRI*
(TRANSLATED BY HANAN AL-SHAYKH)

God is the light of the heavens and the earth.
His light may be likened to a niche
where a lamp stands.
The lamp within glass that glitters like a star
lit by a Holy Tree, by
an olive that is neither
from the East nor the West.
Even its oil would shine, whether or not fire touched it.
Light upon Light.
God draws to His light whom He will.

—*THE KORAN 24:35*

God reveals Himself in creation
and in the human soul.

By entering into his heart man discovers
not only that he can love God,
but that he is loved by God.

The Cosmic Mystery itself is
beyond words,
beyond thought.

It is an inexpressible mystery,
manifesting itself in the cosmos;
infinitely transcendent
and not to be uttered.

The whole creation is filled
with the presence of God.

—Dom Bede Griffiths, in The Cosmic Revelation

Truth is perfect and complete in itself.
Truth is timeless.
Truth isn't far away: it's nearer than near.
You don't have to attain it; you have it.
Don't look to other people for advice.
Instead, learn how to listen deep within your own self.
In this way, body and mind become a single unity
and you will also understand the unity of all things.

Everyday thinking may well stop you
entering the palace of wisdom.

Your search in the pages of books,
finding your way through the thickets of other people's words,
may bring you knowledge,
but it won't necessarily help you to find
the reflection of your true self.

When you no longer feel so impressed by what
the mind constructs,
your original self will appear,
in all its completeness.

Cultivate an awareness of mind while you still can.
Life is short.
You will discover a treasure-trove of wisdom.
You can share this in turn with others.
You can bring to others happiness and peace.

—Dogen Zenji

To say that I am made in the image of God
is to say that love is the reason for my existence,
for God is love.
Love is my true identity.
Selflessness is my true self.
Love is my true character.
Love is my name.

—Thomas Merton

The whole of existence arises in me.
In me arises the threefold world.
This "Everything" is everywhere within me.
The world consists of nothing else.

—Hevajra Tantra

Birds can no longer be seen in the sky.
A last cloud follows them.

We sit together: mountain and me.
Soon, there's only mountain.

—Li Po

Oh God of my ancestors and Lord of mercy,
who has made all things . . .
with you is Wisdom.
She knows and understands what is pleasing in your sight.
And what is right.
Send her forth that she may labor by my side,
guide me sagely in my actions
and guard me with her glory.

—Solomon's Prayer for Wisdom

The beginning of wisdom is a sincere desire to know.
I prayed and understanding was given to me.
I called upon God
and the Spirit of Wisdom came to me.

I loved her beyond health and beauty.
I chose her over light,
for the light she sends can never go out.

For Wisdom, which is the worker of all things, has taught me.
Wisdom is the breath of the power of God.
Wisdom is an unblemished influence flowing from
the Glory of the One.

She is the brightness of the eternal light.
She is the spotless mirror of the power of God,
She is the image of God's goodness.
And being but one, she can do all things.
And remaining in herself, she makes everything new again.

In every age, entering into seeking souls,
she makes them friends of God, and of the prophets.
Oh, she is more beautiful than the sun,
and beyond the majesty of stars.

Comparing her with light, she surpasses light.
I loved her, and sought her out from the time of my youth.
I desired to make her mine, and was a lover of her beauty.

If riches are so desirable in life,
what wealth could be greater than Wisdom,
the catalyst in all things?

—*Adapted from the Wisdom of Solomon, Chapters 6, 7, 8*

There is no great mystery concerning the will of God,
in so far as it applies to our small selves.
God's will is written into His nature,
and the nature of God is love.
Therefore, when we pray in accordance with the law of love,
we are praying in accordance with the will of God.

—*Agnes Sanford*

Be soft in your practice.
Think of the method like a gentle silvery stream,
rather than a powerful waterfall.
Follow the stream.
Trust in its course.
It will make its way,
meandering here, trickling there.
It will find the channels,
the breaks, the clefts.
You have only to follow it.
Keep it in the line of your vision.
Let it carry you.

—SHENG-YEN

Whatever forms are perceptible to your eye draw their
origins from the unseen world.
If form disappears, should this matter?
It came from the Everlasting.
Do not mourn that every form you see, every truth you hear and
value, will vanish.
The divine fountain never ceases to flow.
Why grieve?
. . . When you have finished with this world, your world will be
one of Light.
Go beyond even that.
Go beyond even where angels play.
Go to the Great Ocean, so that the single drop that
you are can become a Sea.

—RUMI

If we cannot make our lives sacred,
well then how can we celebrate the
existence of God on earth?

—*Bem Le Hunte*

Take my life, and let it be
Consecrated, Lord, to thee;
Take my moments and my days,
Let them flow in ceaseless praise.
Take my hands, and let them move
At the impulse of thy love.
Take my feet, and let them be
Swift and beautiful for thee.
Take my voice, and let me sing
Always, only, for my King.
Take my lips, and let them be
Filled with messages from thee.
Take my silver and my gold,
Not a mite would I withhold.
Take my intellect, and use
every power as thou shalt choose.
Take my will, and make it thine;
It shall be no longer mine.
Take my heart, it is thine own;
It shall be thy royal throne.
Take my love: my Lord, I pour
At thy feet its treasure store.
Take myself, and I will be,
Ever, only, all for thee.

—*Frances Ridley Havergal*

In the One, there are the many,
while through the many is to be found the One.

—*Jean Houston*

It is written:
You shall be holy, as
I am holy.

—*1 Peter 1:16*

The important thing,
the thing that lies before me . . .
is to absorb into my nature all that has been done to me,
to make it part of me,
to accept it without complaint, fear or reluctance.

It is only by realizing what I am
that I have found comfort of any kind.

To regret one's own experience is
to arrest one's own development.
To deny one's own experience is to put a lie
into the lips of one's own life.
It is no less than a denial of the soul.

—*Oscar Wilde, in De Profundis*

As there is no screen or ceiling between our
heads and the infinite
heavens, so there is no bar or wall in the soul where we, the effect,
cease, and God, the cause, begins.

I am constrained every moment to acknowledge a
higher origin for events
than the will I call mine.

There is deep power in which we exist and whose
beatitude is accessible to us.
Every moment when the individual feels invaded by it is
memorable.

It comes to the lowly and simple; it comes to
whosoever will put off
what is foreign and proud; it comes as insight;
it comes as serenity and grandeur.
The soul's health consists in the fullness of its reception.

For ever and ever the influx of this better and
more universal self is new and unsearchable.

Within us is the soul of the whole: the wise silence, the universal
beauty, to which every part and particle is equally related;
the eternal One.

When it breaks through our intellect, it is genius;
when it breathes
through our will, it is virtue; when it flows through
our affections, it is love.

—*Ralph Waldo Emerson*

You have created us
for yourself.
And our hearts are restless, Lord,
until they rest in you.

—*Augustine of Hippo*

Deep in the heart of every being,
I make my home.
From me comes memory and knowledge.
And an end to indifference.

—*Bhagavad Gita 15:15*

To cling too tenaciously to the "self"
and its own fulfilment would guarantee
that there would be no fulfilment at all.

—*Thomas Merton*

Holy One: You are my lover.
You are my stream that runs!
You are my sun!
Make me your reflection.

—*Mechthild of Magdeburg*

Know God.

Then your doubts about who you are can fall away.
When you are no longer "just" your body,
when you also know your eternal self,
your ideas about birth and death will change. . . .

Know God is alive in your heart.
Always.
Truly, there's not much more to know in this life.

Pause and reflect.
You can experience that the whole world is
full of God.

The Self is hidden in the hearts of everyone,
just as butter is hidden in cream.
This is the highest teaching.

—*Shvetashvatara Upanishad 1:11, 12, 16; 2:16*

PRAYERS
THAT HEAL

One of the most challenging questions we can ask ourselves is "Do I really *want* to be well?" or, "Do I truly want to be healed?" This deserves your most serious consideration, especially in a world where powerlessness is normalized and the desire for a quick superficial "fix" is rampant.

To be "well" is not dependent solely on physical strength. You need to respect and care for your body—and appreciate it. That means eating well, working hard, resting when you need to, participating wholeheartedly in life, and consciously limiting or excluding what may bring fleeting pleasure but lasting harm. It also means being selective about what you take into your mind: what you think and talk about; the company you keep; the books you read or media you watch; and, yes, the prayers you say.

The story of "being well" and of healing, though, doesn't end there. *With a spiritually formed vision of healing, we can be increasingly well to our last breath.* But such a vision demands that we give up the illusion that life should run entirely on our agenda. It also asks us to cooperate in a world of "wellness" and healing that goes far beyond our individual selves. And it particularly requires us to give up any lingering desire to hurt or harm others or ourselves—*or wish them to be harmed.*

This is where we see prayer as our most faithful friend. No longer relying solely on our ego strengths or temperament, we can turn within to find new depths in our soul's strengths. We can be *present* to and for ourselves in ways that are unconditionally healing. We can become good company for ourselves as well as others. Our resourcefulness can be illuminated by compassion.

That prayer *can* and does heal is a small daily miracle. And if it does not always heal in ways that match our current agenda, it can unfailingly heal us when it comes to attitude and outlook.

Forgiveness is a powerful example of this. Only a few of the prayers in this collection refer to forgiveness explicitly, but many offer a way *to reconcile with the truth of a particular situation and to meet it and transform your experience of it with wisdom and love.*

Those words lie on the page in innocence, yet they can literally make life worth living all over again. They remind us that we can heal suffering, and cause far less of it.

This isn't always easy. But the alternatives are far harder! To pray for healing—for wellness, wisdom and greater love—is an act of courage and humility. Beauty emerges from that. So does truth. *Asking,* we receive. "Seek," said that inclusive and most loving of healers, Jesus of Nazareth. "Seek. *And you will find.*"

Healing is of the essence of spirituality,
and all real healing is spiritual.

—THOMAS MOORE

If "suffering" is not a repairing process,
I will make it so.
I will learn the lesson it teaches.
These are not idle words.
These are not the consolations of the sick.

Life is a mystery.
The fearful pain will fade.
I must turn to work.
I must put my agony into something,
change it.
"Sorrow shall be changed into joy."

It is to lose oneself more utterly,
to love more deeply,
to feel oneself part of life—not separate.
Oh Life! accept me—make me worthy—teach me.

—KATHERINE MANSFIELD

The world is new to us every morning.
This is God's gift,
and every person should believe
that they are reborn each day.

—BA'AL SHEM TOV

May peace come to all who act with evil intent,
and may there be an end to all vengeance
and to all talk of punishment and chastisement.

Horrors mock all who have been among us,
exceeding the boundaries of human comprehension,
and the martyrs are numerous.

Thus, O God,
don't weigh their suffering with the scales
of your justice,
and don't require a grim reckoning,
but rather take account of them differently:

Let all the hangmen prosper
together with all who are traitors and spies
and all who are evil,
and forgive them
on account of the courage and soulfulness of others.
Take note of all the good they have done,
and not the evil.

And in the remembrance of our enemies,
may we no longer live as their victims,
nor as their nightmares and horrid apparitions,
but rather may we come to their assistance
so that they might turn from their madness.

Only this will be required of them
so that we, when all is over and done,
might live as human beings among others,

so that peace once more might break forth upon this earth
for all who are of good will,
and so that this peace might come to the others as well.

—*A PRAYER SAID TO HAVE BEEN LEFT BEHIND*

AT RAVENSBURG CONCENTRATION CAMP.

(TRANSLATED BY MARK S. BURROWS)

I am here only to be truly helpful.
I am here to represent Him who sent me.
I do not have to worry about what to say or what to do,
because He Who sent me will direct me.
I am content to be wherever He wishes,
knowing He goes there with me.
I will be healed
as I let Him teach me to heal.

—FROM A COURSE IN MIRACLES

O death, where is thy sting?
O grave, where is thy victory?
. . . Beloved brothers and sisters,
stand steady and firm.
Stand in the fullness of your godly efforts.

—*1 CORINTHIANS 15:55, 58*

I have put before you life and death,
blessings and curses.
Choose life!

Choose life so that you and your descendants
may live.

—*Deuteronomy 30:19*

The Lord is my shepherd.
I shall not want.
He makes me lie down in green pastures.
He leads me beside still waters.
He restores my soul.
He shows me where I should walk,
choosing the path that witnesses his name.

And though I walk through the valley
of the shadow of death,
I will fear no harm.
You are with me.
Your rod and your staff comfort me.
You prepare a table for me
within sight of those who are called my enemies.
You anoint my head with oil.
My cup runs over.
Goodness and mercy will surely follow me
all the days I am alive.
And I will live forever in the
house of the Eternal.

—*Psalm 23*

Every tree, every growing thing
as it grows, affirms one truth:
you harvest what you sow.
With life as fleeting as a half-drawn breath,
you have no need to plant anything but love.

All that you can see has its roots in the unseen.
Forms change; essence remains.
Every sight will vanish, however gorgeous.
Every word will fade, however sweet.
But be strong of heart!
Where they come from is everlasting.
And renewing.

If God spoke and said,
"Rumi, give due to all that has brought you to my arms,"
there would be not a single thought, feeling or action
that would not cause me to bow down.

—*Rumi*

Today, sweet Holy Spirit, I can't pray.
I am dry.
Like a leaf that once was green and is turning to dust
I can do nothing more than sit in your presence
and, bringing to mind your stillness,
let myself be stilled.

—*S.D.*

Oneness of life and light,
trusting in your unconditional compassion,
I ask you to end my ignorance.
Transform me into an instrument of Love.

May I be medicine for the sick and weary.
May I become food and drink for those who starve.

May I protect the powerless and the poor.
May I be a lamp for those who need your Light.

May I be shelter for those who need safety.
May I guide all seekers to the Other Shore.

May all grow in happiness through my actions,
and let no one suffer because of what I do.

Whether they love or hate me,
whether they protect or injure me,
may all beings realize true surrender
and Supreme Nirvana.

Namo-Amida-Buddha
[I trust in the Buddha of Infinite Light]

—METTA KARUNA, PRAYER OF COMPASSION

Let us pray for peace of mind and healing of hearts
wherever that is needed.
Let's pray especially for those in our world
who are feeling lost or abandoned:
we can be with them.
Let's pray for those in our world who are suffering
from religious prejudice or violence:
we can be with them.

Let's pray for the children in our world who lack safekeeping:
we can be with them.
Let's pray for all those in our world in need of respect,
safety and justice:
we can be with them.
Let's pray for those in our world who are grieving . . . who are
enduring physical or mental pain . . . or who are facing or
enduring losses:
we can be with them.
Let's pray for the peacemakers of our world, the healers and the
joyful ones, those who ease our lives and make them lighter,
more glorious and more meaningful:
we can be with them.
Let's pray for all those who will come into our world today . . . and
all those who will leave it:
we can be with them.
Let's pray for our own selves . . . our families . . . the small and
large communities of which we are part . . . for our whole
human family:
we can be with them.
Finally, let's pray for those spiritual guides and teachers whose
words, loving-kindness and example allow us to find our way:
we can be with them.
Blessed be.

—*S.D.*

No amount of prayer or meditation
will achieve what helping others can.

—MEHER BABA

Out of the depths, I cry to you O Lord.

Lord: hear my voice!

Hear my pleas!

If you were to judge us by our shortcomings, Lord,

who would remain standing?

But you can forgive.

And we are in awe.

I wait for you.

My soul seeks you.

More eagerly than

those who wait for the sun to rise

on a new dawn,

I ready myself for you.

Let those who seek to know,

anticipate you in increasing stillness.

Because, with you, kindness comes.

And the fullness of healing.

—*PSALM 130:1–7*

Out of the depths of my soul I cry,

Jesus draw nigh,

Jesus draw nigh.

Lord lend an ear to my earnest pleading,

speak to my soul,

O Lord,

to mend and make whole!

—*TRADITIONAL AFRICAN-AMERICAN GOSPEL SONG*

My grace is sufficient for you.

—WORDS OF JESUS, 2 CORINTHIANS 12:9

May I open to the ease and comfort of God's grace.
May I remember the quiet times when something
shifted within me, and I grew in grace.

May I remember the moments of kindness when
my heart opened, and I grew in grace.

May I remember when I reached beyond my own
worries to help another, and I grew in grace.

May I remember the times of darkness when inspiration arose,
and I grew in grace.

May our world be filled with moments of grace.
May we bring grace to life through our daily actions.
May everyone live in grace, happiness and peace.
May I live in grace, happiness and peace.
May I embody grace.

—S.D.

First Noble Truth: *In life there is suffering.*
We free ourselves whenever we ask:
"How can I help?"

—*S.D.*

You, O Love,
are the most ancient of all . . .
In every expression of goodness, O Love,
we see your face.

—*FROM THE ATHARVA VEDA*

Pay no attention to harsh words that
others speak.
Don't concern yourself with what others
have done—
or have not done.
Observe your own actions and inactions.

Take care of what you are creating through:
right action,
right speech,
right livelihood.

—*THE DHAMMAPADA 4:7, 12*

Let me see things as they truly are.

Let me know:
I am a part of an infinite Whole.
I belong to a vast human family.

I affect others as much as others affect me.
I am free to live for the benefit and harmony of all.

Let me know:
I can make my choices wisely.
I can silence my criticisms and create peace.
I can remove myself from harm without causing harm.
I can seek to understand beliefs that are different from mine.
I can see the whole person and not just what impacts on me.
I can view others through the eyes of forgiveness and compassion.
I can offer others the priceless gifts of peace.

Let me know:
I can contribute to a world where diversity is celebrated.
I can offer respect, interest and safety as daily gifts.
I can be accepting of all those whose lives touch mine.
I can be grateful for my experiences, without exception.

Let me now envision:
A world where every person is free to live fully,
seeking and finding love, harmony and peace,
while dancing to the music of life!

May these words benefit us,
and all those whom our lives touch.

—*S.D.*

When conflict occurs,
let yourself remember the Mind of Compassion.
Help all beings.
Step into the conflict. Restore peace.

—*Adapted from the Vimalakirti Nirdesa Sutra*

When practising mindfulness,
don't be dominated by the distinction
between good and evil,
thus creating a battle within oneself.
Whenever a wholesome thought arises,
acknowledge it.
Whenever an unwholesome thought arises,
acknowledge it.
To acknowledge it, is enough.

—THICH NHAT HANH, IN THE MIRACLE OF MINDFULNESS

Grant us peace and harmony, O God,
and assist us always to preserve union and charity
in the midst of our diversity, differences and difficulties.
May the sun never set on our anger.
Rather, may a spirit of reconciliation dwell among us.
Through our experience of your forgiving love
may we have the grace
both to forgive those who have hurt us
and to seek pardon
from those whom we have offended.
Be with us as we come and go,
so that our hearts may always be centred in you.

We ask this through Jesus,
the gracious sign of your love and forgiveness.
Amen.

—CATHERINE MCCAULEY

May my words today heal myself and others.
May my words today calm myself and others.
May my words today bring insight for myself and others.
May my words today express and affirm the very best
of who I am, of who others are.
May my words today uplift our world and bring comfort
to all who live in it.

—S.D.

Grandfather,
Sacred One,
teach us love, compassion, honor,
that we may heal the earth
and heal each other.

—TRADITIONAL OJIBWAY PRAYER

When my yearning for the Friend gathered sufficient pace,
everything else became meaningless.
The Beloved had no interest in my excuses.
I tossed them out—
and discovered silence.

The rationality I'd worshipped became boring.
No choice but to bid it goodbye.
Old thinking gone, silent, blissful:
My days pass
with my head
resting at the feet
of my Beloved.

—ABU SA'ID ABUL-KHAYR

Do you want long life and happiness?
Strive for peace with all your heart.

—*Psalm 34:12, 14*

If you are a genuine human being,
gamble everything for Love!
If you are not,
then leave this gathering.

—*Rumi*

Beloved, let us love one another:
for love is of God.
And all who love are born of God,
and know God.
Those who love not, know not God;
for God is love.

None of us has seen God at any time.
Yet, if we love one another,
God lives within us,
and love is perfected within us.

—*1 John 4:7–8, 12*

Let me not pray just to be saved from dangers,
but to be fearless in facing them.
Let me not cry out for an end to my pain,
but for the courage to bear it.

Let me not look for allies in the struggles of life,
but toward my own strengths.
Let me not crave to be saved from fear,
but for the patience to claim my freedom.
Grant that I may not be cowardly,
experiencing Your mercy only when I am strong;
but let me also know the touch of Your hand
in my weakness.

—ADAPTED FROM RABINDRANATH TAGORE

The following prayer restores cooperation in a time of conflict, especially between people who know one another well. It is also powerful for any group, culture or nation that might see those with different views or experiences as "other." Please allow time for silent reflection.

Beloved,
we ask for the grace and humility to remember
that what we share with _____ is more vital than whatever
may hinder or divide us.
"We" want love; so do "they."
"We" want safety, trust, respect and peace; so do "they."
"We," "they": all yours.
All yours.
Help us to find a way forward that benefits all.
Help us to think calmly and wisely with concern for all.
Help us to move through this challenging situation
and find the rewards of wisdom and peace on the other side.
We pray this, trusting in your inspiration.
Blessed be.

—S.D.

O heavenly Father,
protect and bless all things
that have breath;
guard them from all evil
and let them sleep in peace.

—ALBERT SCHWEITZER

Conquer the one who is angry with love.
Conquer the one who is bitter with goodness.
Conquer the one who is mean with generosity.
Conquer the one who deceives herself with truth.

Speak truthfully.
Master your emotions.
Share whatever you have.
These are the three steps of liberation.

—THE DHAMMAPADA 17:3–4

Let me tell you what the Middle Way is.
Dressing in worn and dirty garments,
letting your hair grow matted,
giving up eating fish or meat:
this won't purify anyone who's deluded.

Nor does mortifying your body through excessive penance let you
triumph over your senses.
All self-inflicted suffering is quite useless
if it remains self-focused.
Give up obsessing about yourself.

Eat and drink according to the needs of your body.
Attachment to appetites
—whether you deprive yourself of them or indulge them—
leads to slavery.
Satisfying the needs of daily life isn't wrong.
To keep your physical self in good health is a duty.
Without this, your mind will not stay strong and clear.
This is the Middle Way.

—*The Buddha, Discourse II*

All over the world the supreme Spirit
has left signs of his presence.

—*Dom Bede Griffiths*

Silence is God's first language;
everything else is a poor translation.
In order to hear that language,
we must learn to be still
and to rest in God.

—*Thomas Keating*

Of all things on earth,
silence most resembles God.

—*Meister Eckhart*

Gracious One, Divine Mother of all that lives,
We call out to you to guide your children.

Bless our eyes, that we may see each other with love.
Bless our ears, that we may hear each other with understanding.
Bless our mouths, that we may speak to each other with
compassion.
Bless our hands, that they may heal, not harm.
Bless our feet, that we may walk beside each other in peace.

Great Spirit, Mother of birth, death and rebirth,
Spirit of the green Earth that feeds us,
Of the creatures that roam upon its surface,
And the tides that lap its shores.

Holy One, let all your children drink of its wisdom
And know that all names of the Divine are but one Name,
And all worship but a dance to the singular music of Life.

—*A PRAYER HONORING THE DIVINE FEMININE*

The Lord showed me, so that I did see clearly,
that He did not dwell in these temples
which men had commanded and set up,
but in people's hearts . . .
His people were His temple,
and He dwelt in them . . .
Be patterns. Be examples
in all countries, places, islands, nations, wherever you come;
that your carriage and life may preach among all sorts of people.
And to them.

Then you will come to walk cheerfully over the world
answering that of God in every one;
whereby in them you may be a blessing,
and make the witness of God in them to bless you.

—George Fox

We call ourselves a utilitarian age,
and we do not know
the uses of any single thing.
We have forgotten that
Water can cleanse, and
Fire purify, and
that the Earth is mother to us all . . .

Still, I am conscious that
behind all this Beauty,
satisfying though it be,
there is some Spirit hidden
of which
the painted forms and shapes are
but modes of manifestation, and
it is with this Spirit that
I desire to become in harmony.

—Oscar Wilde, in De Profundis

The kingdom is inside you,
and outside you.
When you know who you are,
you will be known.

What you will know is that you are
children of an eternal father, mother, all that is.
If you do not know who you are
you live in poverty, you are poverty.

Know what's right in front of you.
What's hidden will be revealed.
There's nothing hidden that won't be revealed.

Don't speak deceitfully.
Don't do what you would hate.
There's nothing hidden that won't be revealed.
Where the beginning is, the end will be.
Blessings on you who stand at the beginning.
You will know the end.
You will live forever.

—From the Gospel of Thomas 3, 5, 6, 18

Where my feet take me: there You are.
Where my thoughts take me: there You are.
Only You! Everywhere.
You. You. You!
When I am happy. You!
When I am bereft. You!
Only You! Everywhere.
You are sky.
You are earth.
You are above.
You are below.
In every beginning.
In every ending.
Only You.

—*Adapted from Rabbi Levi Yitzchak*

O my God! O my God!
Unite the hearts of Thy servants,
and reveal to them Thy great purpose.
May they follow Thy commandments
and abide in Thy law.
Help them, O God,
in their endeavor,
and grant them strength to serve Thee.
O God! Leave them not to themselves,
but guide their steps by the light of Thy Knowledge,
and cheer their hearts by Thy love.
Verily, Thou art their Helper and their Lord.

—*Baha'u'llah*

Holy Spirit,
Giver of life,
Animating all,
Sustaining all,
Cleansing all,
Washing away errors,
Healing wounds,
You are our Life!
Luminous.
Marvellous.
You awaken the heart
from its ancient sleep.

—*Hildegard of Bingen*

If anyone upsets you,
get on with your day with a light heart.
If everyone behaves that way,
ignore what they say.
Nothing's new in that kind of talk.
The wind will blow it all away!

Or if they want to close you off from God
and say (to flatter you),
"Oh how wonderful you are!",
then turn your back on that talk too.
The wind will blow it all away!

—*Adapted from the teaching of Marguerite de Navarre*

I *am* a soul, and I *have* a body.
I am non-physical, eternal . . .
I express myself in different ways through my body,
but I exist in my own right.

—B. K. SISTER JAYANTI

Give up anger.
Give up pride.
You liberate yourself from unhappiness
when your emotions do not enslave you.

Overcome anger with a commitment to peace.
Overcome wrongdoing by doing right.
Overcome selfishness with generosity.

Speak the truth.
Stay calm.
Give generously.
These three steps will lead you to Nirvana.

—THE DHAMMAPADA 17

You are on the path.
You have your lamp.
The map is unfolding.
Go forward in trust.

—S.D.

I live
in the spaciousness of
God's perfect peace.

—S.D.

God of stillness and
creative action,
help us to find space
for quietness today
that we may live
creatively,
discover the inner
meaning of silence,
and learn the
wisdom
that heals the world.

Send peace and joy
to each quiet place,
to all who are
waiting
and listening.
And to those who neither
wait nor listen and scarcely dare even hope.

May your still small
voice be heard
through the Great Silence,
in the love of the Spirit.
Amen.

—*MARY HOLIDAY*

When Lady Julian of Norwich asked Jesus during a vision how we should
deal with our sorrows and problems, Jesus replied:

I can make all things well.
I know how to make all things well.
I want to make all things well.
I will make all things well, and you will see with your own eyes
that every kind of thing will be well . . .
All will be well.
All will be well.
And all manner of things will be well.

—LADY JULIAN OF NORWICH

As different streams,
having their sources in different places,
all mingle their water in the sea,
so, O Lord,
the different paths which our human family takes
through different tendencies,
various though they appear,
crooked or straight,
all lead to Thee.

—SWAMI VIVEKANANDA

This existence of ours passes as quickly as autumn clouds.
To watch the birth and death of beings
is to see the movements of a dance.
A lifetime is no more than a flash of lightning
in the sky,
tumbling like a torrent
down a steep mountain.

—THE BUDDHA

. . . In the Whole, everything is already numbered.
When anyone falls, that perfect sum is not lessened.
Whoever lets go in his fall, dives into the source.
And is healed . . .
. . . Waves, Marina, we are ocean!
Depths, Marina, we are sky.
Earth, Marina, we are earth, Spring a thousand times over . . .
. . . Praising, my dear one—let us be reckless with praise.
Nothing is truly ours.

—RAINER MARIA RILKE

Lord, make me an instrument of your peace.

Where there is hatred, let me bring love;

where there is injury, pardon;

where there is doubt, faith;

where there is despair, hope;

where there is darkness, light;

and where there is sadness, joy.

O Divine Master, grant that I may not so much seek

to be comforted, as to comfort others;

to be understood, as to understand;

to be loved, as to love.

For it is in giving to others that we ourselves receive;

it is in pardoning others that we ourselves are pardoned;

and it is in dying to this world that we are born to eternal life.

Amen

—PRAYER ATTRIBUTED TO FRANCIS OF ASSISI

Let me have the courage to see things as they are.
Let me see the beauty.
Let me see the suffering.
Let me see the peace.
Let me see the turmoil.
Let me see the light.
Let me see the darkness.
Let me see the agitation.
Let me see the stillness.

Accepting myself in my wholeness,
may I extend the same grace to others.

I am willing to trust the wholeness of who I am.
I need not disown or hide any part of myself.
I welcome the peace that such inner harmony will bring.

In coming to a greater peace within myself,
I can accept others.

This is my vow:
I offer peace to myself,
and to all beings.
I choose to embody peace.
I choose to live peace.
I choose to be peace.

—S.D.

To study the Way is to study the self.
To study the self is to forget the self.
To forget the self
is to be enlightened by everything in the universe.
To be enlightened by everything in the universe
is to be free of the mind, the body, the self,
and those of others.
Even thoughts of enlightenment are gone.
Life continues.

—DOGEN ZENJI

The Lord of Love said, "Let me be many!"
And in the depths of his meditation,
he created everything that exists.
Meditating, he entered into all.
The One who has no form, took many forms.
The infinite One embraced the finite.
The One who is placeless, found places.
The One who is wisdom, allowed ignorance.
The One who is real, caused the unreal.
It is he who becomes everything.
It is he who gives life to all.
. . . It is he who fills every heart with joy.

—FROM THE TAITTIRIYA UPANISHAD 6:1, 7:1

Give ear, O Lord, unto our prayer,
and attend to the voice of our supplication.
Make us poor in spirit: that ours may be the kingdom of heaven.
Make us to mourn for sin: that we may be comforted by thy grace.
Make us meek: that we may inherit the earth.
Make us to hunger and thirst after righteousness:
that we may be filled therewith.
Make us merciful: that we may obtain mercy.
Make us pure in heart: that we may see thee.
Make us peacemakers: that we may be called thy children.
Make us willing to be persecuted for righteousness' sake:
that our reward may be great in heaven.

—Book of Common Order

PRAYERS OF CELEBRATION

The most common images of prayer are of heads bowed and voices hushed. Or of someone sitting or kneeling quietly with eyes closed, turning inward. Those surely can be restorative, even healing experiences. Yet the repertoire of prayer extends so naturally into the most joyous, exuberant moments of life also. Better still, a simple daily prayer can lift an everyday experience into a sacred one. It can create ritual out of the most routine moments, and bring you to an awareness of the sacred that adds the most precious dimension to your life and how you regard it.

A life grounded in prayer also *gives* you much to celebrate. It heightens your awareness of your place in an awesome, infinite universe. It brings you awareness of yourself as soul or spirit, as well as body, mind and feelings. It lets you see with gratitude what others do for you. And with the fullness that prayer brings, it makes it so much easier to give without feeling depleted.

Because prayer is a contemplative act, it also lets you look "deeply" or mindfully—and supports you to appreciate more fully what you see. Celebratory prayers in particular invite your increased participation in life, as well as your vigor and enthusiasm. And whether said alone or with others, such prayers bring an exquisite reminder that you belong to a vast human family transcending all borders and divisions, and extending back beyond recorded time.

This is literally energizing, and it is no surprise that many people experience the prayerful acts of song, dance or even communal service and hospitality as particularly inspirational.

At the spiritually inclusive services I lead at a big inner-city church in Sydney, where multifaith and multicultural expectations are taken for granted in a particularly twenty-first-century way, we regularly have short readings from what we call "our shared spiritual inheritance." This means that while we honor and respect the source of the prayers or teachings we are hearing, we do not see any truly loving prayer or teaching as "belonging" in an exclusive way to any one group, culture or religion. We see such prayers as messages to be treasured by all seekers on the path of love. Sufi poet Kabir expresses this sublimely:

Inside Love is more joy than you could begin to understand.
Even when the sky is cloudless, rain pours down.
There are entire rivers of light.
The universe is charged with a single kind of love.

[My favorite blessing follows, a daily, sometimes hourly gift that is an honor to share with you.]

May the blessings of God rest upon you.
May God's peace abide with you.
May God's presence illuminate your hearts,
now and forever more.

—HAZRAT INAYAT KHAN

I find you in all these things that I care for easily,
like a brother.
In modest things,
you are seed.
To what is powerful,
you give immense power.

It is a marvelous game
that strength plays,
serving through things,
growing through roots,
refining through tree trunks,
and in the highest branches rising—
like a resurrection.

—RAINER MARIA RILKE

Though I speak with the tongues of men and of angels,
and have not charity,
I am become as sounding brass, or a tinkling cymbal.
And though I have the gift of prophecy,
and understand all mysteries, and all knowledge;
and though I have all faith,
so that I could remove mountains,
and have not charity,
I am nothing.
And though I bestow all my goods to feed the poor,
and though I give my body to be burned,
and have not charity,
it profiteth me nothing.
Charity suffereth long, and is kind;
charity envieth not;
charity vaunteth not itself,
is not puffed up.
Doth not behave itself unseemly,
seeketh not her own,
is not easily provoked,
thinketh no evil;
Rejoiceth not in iniquity,
but rejoiceth in the truth;
Beareth all things,
believeth all things,
hopeth all things, endureth all things.
Charity never faileth . . .
. . . When that which is perfect is come,
then that which is in part shall
be done away.

When I was a child, I spake as a child,
I understood as a child,
I thought as a child:
but when I became a man,
I put away childish things.
For now we see through a glass darkly;
but then face to face:
now I know in part;
but then shall I know even as also I am known.
And now abideth faith, hope, charity, these three;
but the greatest of these is charity.

—*1 Corinthians 13:1–8, 10–13*
(King James Version)

In the beginning, God created the heavens and the earth.
The earth had no form then.
And darkness was on the face of the deep.
And the Spirit of God moved there upon the face of the waters.
And God said, "Let there be light." And there was light.
God saw the light. And that it was good.

—*Genesis 1:1–4*

Holy, Holy, Holy, Lord of all,
heaven and earth are filled with your glory.

Blessed is he who comes in the name of the Lord.
Hosanna in the highest.

—*Isaiah 6:3; Matthew 21:9*

(The soul speaks to God)
You are my lover, Lord.
You are my yearning.
You are my stream that flows.
You are my sun.
I?
I am your reflection.

(God speaks to the soul)
It is my very nature that makes me love you.
For I, I am love itself.
It is my very yearning that makes me love you unutterably.
That yearning to be loved from your heart.
I?
I am eternal.

—MECHTHILD OF MAGDEBURG

Raise your voices joyfully to the Lord,
all you who live on this earth.
Worship the Lord with your delight.
Come into the presence of the Divine singing!

Know this:
that the Lord is God,
that he made you,
that you are his,
that each of you can be called,
"His people,"
flock of his pasture.

Enter his gates with gratitude.
Enter his courts with praise.

Give thanks!
Praise his name!

For the Lord is good.
His kindness is unceasing.
His truth is without beginning or end.

—*Psalm 100*

Behold!
I bring you tidings of great joy
which shall be for everyone.

—*Luke 2:10*

Joy
is the unmistakable sign
of the presence of God.

—*Teilhard de Chardin*

From Joy I came.
For Joy I live.
Into Thy sacred joy
I will dissolve again.

—*Paramahamsa Yogananda*

All this is full. All that is full.
From fullness comes fullness.
When fullness is taken from fullness,
fullness remains.
OM shanti, shanti, shanti.

The Self is one.
Unmoving, it moves faster than thoughts.
It moves faster than feelings.
Though motionless, no one can outrun it.
Without the Self, life could not exist.

The Self appears to move . . . but remains still.
The Self seems far away . . . but is always near.
The Self is within all.
The Self transcends all.

Those for whom the Self is transcendent only,
live in darkness.
Those for whom the Self is immanent only,
live in greater darkness still.
But those who know the Self
as both transcendent and immanent,
can approach the sea of death fearlessly.

Source of life for all creatures,
spread your light!
Mute your dazzling splendor
so that I can see your holy Self,
even that very Self that I am!

—*Adapted from the Isha Upanishad 1, 1:4–5, 12–14, 16*

How lovely are the places where you dwell,
Lord of hosts!
My soul longs, my soul aches to enter
your presence.
Spirit and flesh cry out with joy
to the living God.

Just as the sparrow finds its home,
and the swallow, a nest where she may lay her young,
so have I found your altars,
Lord of Hosts, Highest Good, my God!

Blessed are those who live knowing you.
Their lives unfold in constant praise.
Blessed are those who trust
in you, whose heart is the highway to Zion.
They go from strength to strength.

O Lord of Hosts, hear my prayer!
Look on the face of those who seek you.
A day with you is like a thousand spent elsewhere.
I would rather be at the threshold of the house of my God
than luxuriating in the tents of ignorance.
For you are Sun, Shield, Grace, Honor.
You withhold nothing from those who
strive with integrity.

O Lord of Hosts,
those who find their comfort in you,
know bliss.

—*PSALM 84*

I sit at a window that's filled with moon.
With my ears I watch the mountain.
With my eyes I hear the stream.
Each molecule preaches a perfect way.
Each moment chants a true sutra:
The most fleeting thought is timeless,
A single hair is all it takes to stir the sea.

—*SHUTAKU*

When you realise how perfect everything is
you will tilt your head back
and laugh at the sky.

—*THE BUDDHA*

Beloved sisters and brothers,
you whom I love and long for,
you, my joy and my crown,
be confident in the Lord!

. . . Rejoice in the Lord always!
Let me say again: Rejoice!
Let your gentleness be known far and wide.
The Lord is with you.

Don't worry about anything.
But in everything you must do,
with prayer and trust,
make what you need known to God.

And the peace of God,
which surpasses anything our human minds can comprehend,
will protect your minds,
will protect your hearts,
will protect you.

—*Philippians 4:1, 4–7*

There is no other way to love but generously.
Love treasures who you are.
Love brings depth and joy to the life
you are continuously creating.

Love opens you to all that you can do and be.
Love makes it easy to receive.
Love lives through acts and actions:
kindness, respect, delight, trust, safety.

Love finds what's good and speaks of it.
Love knows what to overlook.
And the value of silence.

Love laughs loudly and often.
Love is daring, as well as kind.
Love seeks and offers beauty.
Love is subtle. And discerning.

Love thinks easily of others.
Love listens with an open mind.
Love is loyal and respectful.
Love gives thanks, and is thankful.

Love honors freedom.
Love does not cling.
Love seeks to understand.
In love, there are no opponents.
Love wishes the best for the other, always.
And even when it is afraid of the answer,
love asks what that best might be.

Love brings quiet patience.
Love makes things right.
Love affirms difference and diversity.
Love makes you vulnerable.
Love mends wounded hearts.

Love belongs to no one and to everyone.
Love lets bad times pass and treasures good times.
Love brings you into the present moment.
Love is a commitment and a calling.
Love never dies.

—*S.D., Adapted from* The Universal Heart

The essential work of a spiritual teacher is
just this—not to tell us what to do but to help
us see who we are.

—*Laurence Freeman*

Love is my religion and my faith.
When my eyes beheld the face of our Friend,
my sorrows became joys.

I can no longer call myself "I".
I can longer call anyone "you".
It makes no sense.

Since I found the love of our Friend
this world and the world to come are one.
If you ask about the eternal beginning
or end—
these are my night and day.

No longer do I grieve
or allow my heart to be clouded.
I have heard Truth's voice.
The union I celebrate is my own.

—Yunus Emre

Divine Radiance,
life-giving Light that shines
throughout the universes;
You who are beyond mortality and the true Self,
You who are Source of all life and power,
Who frees the soul from all that grieves us,
we pour out our devotion to you.

We meditate upon the Light that transforms darkness.
We meditate upon the Light that brings an end to ignorance.
We meditate upon the Light radiating at the heart of all creation:
the Light that is within us.

We call upon our own true nature,
the Divine Light within us,
to move us beyond illusion.
We call upon the Divine Light to enlighten us.
OM *shanti, shanti, shanti*

—*Adapted from the Gayatri Mantra*

The earth is the Lord's and the fullness of it:
the world, and all who dwell in the world.
He established it upon the seas.
And on the tides.

Who will go up to the hill of the Lord?
Who will stand in this holy place?

Those who avoid harm,
those who have peaceful hearts,
those who avoid pride and vanity
will be especially blessed.

Lift up your heads, O ye gates!
And be ye lift up,
You everlasting doors,
and the King of Glory shall come in.

Who is the King of Glory?
The Lord of Hosts.

—*From Psalm 24*

Disguise yourself in a thousand ways:
I will still know you, my Beloved.
Veil yourself with any enchantment:
I will still feel you, most precious Presence,
near and known.

In the springing of cypresses,
in the shining surfaces of lakes,
in the tumult of fountains,
in clouds that roll,
in meadows laced in colour:
I will greet you!

O Beloved Presence,
you who glow more brightly than all the stars combined,
I see your face even in the plants that climb,
in grapes that cluster,
in dawn making the mountains glow red,
in the vast arch of the sky.

You make the whole world glad.
You make every heart great.
You breathe the world.

—*Hafiz*

Let me see myself through the eyes of Love.
Let me honor without conditions my unique, irreplaceable
gift of life.
Let me transform my complaints and judgments.
Let me release my limitations.
Let me find new words to praise the beauty of existence.

Let me meet life with a brave heart.
Let me embrace life's complexity.
Let me embrace life's simplicity.
Let me face my choices, and own them.
Let me accept my responsibilities, and be glad of them.
Let me understand what I owe others.
Let me give to others with less concern about what I am owed.
Let me know
that in caring for others I am also caring for myself.
Let me live as an instrument of Love.
Let me grow in appreciation,
in tolerance, in good humor,
in patience, in forgiveness,
in joy.
Let me be love.
Amen.

—S.D.

Turn away from anything that clouds your thinking.
Let your mind be filled with love!
Let it spread through all corners of the world
so that the whole world,
the world above and the world below,
is filled with love.
Let this love be sublime.
Let this love be beyond measure.
So that love flourishes
everywhere.

—FROM THE DIGHA NIKAYA

I thought Love lived in the hot sunshine,
But O he lives in the moony light!
I thought to find Love in the heat of day,
But sweet Love is the comforter of night.
Seek Love in the pity of others' woe,
In the gentle relief of another's care,
In the darkness of night and the winter's snow,
In the naked and outcast, seek Love there.

—WILLIAM BLAKE

Let nature teach me.
Let nature heal me.

Acting with greater love toward the world,
I will act with greater love toward myself.
Our joy in living depends on love.
We cannot control the physical world.
We are part of the physical world.
It lives in us; we live in it.
What we can control is how we think, choose and behave.
This is my prayer.

Let life flow.
May I touch the earth lightly.
May I cultivate beauty and nourishment wherever I can.

May I use the earth's resources modestly and gratefully.
May I plant thoughtfully, tend, harvest and give thanks.
May I swim in the oceans or rivers with wonder.
May I regard the sky's stars with awe.
May I honor the light of the moon.
May I be warmed by the sun.
May I protect myself and others from what is harsh.
May I stay open to what is tender and renewing.
May I touch and be touched by the life force that we share.
And, most humbly, may I know Spirit in it all.

May all with whom I share this earth live in peace.
Blessed be.

—*S.D.*

If there is to be peace in the world,
there must be peace in the nations.
If there is to be peace in the nations,
there must be peace in the cities.
If there is to be peace in the cities,
there must be peace between neighbors.
If there is to be peace between neighbors,
there must be peace in the home.
If there is to be peace in the home,
There must be peace in the heart.

—*Lao-Tzu*

Joyful, joyful, we adore Thee,
God of glory, Lord of love;
Hearts unfold like flowers before Thee,
opening to the sun above.

Melt the clouds of sin and sadness;
drive the dark of doubt away;
Giver of immortal gladness,
fill us with the light of day!

All Thy works with joy surround Thee,
earth and heaven reflect Thy rays;
Stars and angels sing around Thee,
center of unbroken praise.

Field and forest, vale and mountain,
flowery meadow, flashing sea;
Singing bird and flowing fountain
call us to rejoice in Thee.

Thou art giving and forgiving,
ever blessing, ever blessed,
Wellspring of the joy of living,
ocean depth of happy rest!

Thou our Father, Christ our Brother,
all who live in love are Thine;
Teach us how to love each other,
lift us to the joy divine.

Mortals, join the happy chorus,
which the morning stars began;
Father love is reigning o'er us,
binding all within its span.

Ever singing, march we onward,
victors in the midst of strife,
Joyful music leads us Sunward,
in the triumph song of life.

—WORDS BY HENRY VAN DYKE, FREQUENTLY SUNG TO LUDWIG
VAN BEETHOVEN'S "ODE TO JOY"

A Brahmin named Sangarava went to the river each
morning and evening to bathe, hoping to be cleansed from
whatever sins he may have committed.
Learning of this, the Buddha said, "If bathing in the river could
purify us then all the frogs, turtles, and crocodiles would be
completely free from sin!

"The real lake is the lake of goodness, with grace as its shore.
Clear and undefiled, it soothes all who enter its depths.
Plunge into the waters of goodness.
Learn to swim there."

—FROM THE SAMYUTTA NIKAYA

Make this an "Alleluia" day!
Look at the world through the eyes of love.
Speak up your gratitude.
Celebrate your appreciation.
Silence your complaints.
Choose kindness.
Witness the happiness you bring to others.
Witness the happiness you bring to yourself.
Alleluia!

—S.D.

Wisdom is radiant and unfading.

She is easily perceived by those who love her.

She is quickly found by those who seek her.

To those who desire her, she hastens to make herself known.

Watch for her early, and your difficulties will be less.

Her place is at your gate.

Even to think of her is to mature your understanding.

Tune your minds with hers, and you will have no need to be anxious.

She moves into the world looking for those who look for her.

Graciously, she appears on their path.

And in every thought, she meets them.

—*WISDOM OF SOLOMON 6:12–16*

My soul sings as I praise you, O Lord of life,

My spirit leaps with joy before you, O Bringer of healing.

You turned your gaze upon me, this unexceptional girl.

And all future generations will be calling me blessed.

God's power lives in me.

He has lifted me up.

Holy is his name.

His goodness flows from generation to generation,

It reaches everyone touched by His love.

He has scattered those who were over-filled with pride.

He has filled the hungry with what is most nourishing.

Goodness is renewed constantly in His heart.

As once He revealed Himself to our ancestors,

to Abraham and those who followed Abraham, so

He carries us with Him through all the ages of the earth.

—*MARY'S SONG OF PRAISE, LUKE 1:46–56*

Come, true light.
Come, life eternal.
Come, hidden mystery.
Come, treasure without name.

Come, reality beyond what can be spoken.
Come, joy that is unceasing.
Come, light that never fades.
Come, Raiser of the fallen.
Come, Alone to the alone.

Come, comforter of my soul.
Come, my joy, my infinite delight.
Come, true light.

—SYMEON

O sweet and loving Spirit
when I stay asleep too long
and forget your many blessings
I ask you please to wake me up
and sing your joyful song to me.
You sing silently.
Your song reaches way beyond the reach of words.
Your song expresses more than any one of us could express.
It's in my soul that I hear it . . .
when you wake me up to your presence.

—MECHTHILD OF MAGDEBURG

I am happy before I have a reason.
I am filled with Light even before the sky
can welcome the sun
or farewell the moon.

O dearest ones,
we've been in love with God
always.
What else could Hafiz do but dance?

—*HAFIZ*

Sometimes vestments look like faded shorts.
Sometimes altar cloths look like picnic rugs.
Sometimes chalices look like paper cups.
Sometimes holy water tastes of ocean.
Sometimes music comes from breaking waves.
Sometimes cathedrals rise as cliff tops.

—*S.D.*

Oh Soul Supreme:
You fill us with reminders of You!

You are the fire in the fire.
You are the sun in the sun.
You are the moon in the moon.
You are the entire firmament in the sky.
You are the Soul Supreme.
You are the waters—You!
Creator of all.

You are woman and man,
you are youth and young girl,
you are the bent aged one,
leaning on a stick.
Your face is everywhere.
You are the butterfly.

And the green parrot with red eyes.
You are the noisy thunder, the changing seasons,
The breeze blowing in space
and the silent depths of the oceans.

You have no beginning.
You are timeless.
You are Light.
You are Source of all.

Imperishable, adorable: even your name is beyond beauty.

Let me know more about You!
Let me follow your gentle path!

—ADAPTED FROM THE SHVETASHVATARA UPANISHAD

The Son of man is come to save
what might otherwise be lost.
How else should we think about the Beloved:
Love eternal, my whole Good,
Happiness that is boundless?
I long to be yours alone.
To keep nothing back for myself.
O everlasting Light,
surpassing all created flares,

flash forth your lightning from above,
piercing the intimacies of my heart.
Make clean, make glad, make bright
and make alive my spirit,
with all the powers my spirit has,
that I may hold and be held,—
in ecstasies of joy.

—Thomas à Kempis

If each one of us could make of our heart
a manger,
then Christ could come again
to this earth.

—Angelus Silesius

If a shepherd had a hundred sheep
and one of them wandered away,
does it not make sense that our shepherd would leave the ninety-nine
to go up into the mountains seeking the one that has strayed?

And when that lost sheep is found,
truly would there not be more rejoicing over that one
than over the ninety-nine that were not lost?

In just that same way, your divine Father
will do all that is needed to bring those in his care
back home to safety.

—Matthew 18:11–14

You are the infinite One and the Lord of Shining Light.
You live beyond darkness, beyond night.
Only through knowledge of you can we overcome death.

Our hearts are your dwelling place.
Throughout the universe, there you are.
Infinite, omnipresent, you are smaller than the smallest.
You are greater than the greatest.

When craving no longer has us in its grip,
when sorrow no longer constrains us,
we can seek you freely.
Seeking you, only you, then—with your grace—
your countless expressions in this world
become apparent.

Lord, Creator, creator even of Brahma, god of creation,
Revealer of truths,
Toward you I turn in my longing for freedom.
Toward you, for refuge, with reverence, I come.
Grant us wisdom.
Grant us peace.

—ADAPTED FROM THE UPANISHADIC TRADITION

Not death, not life, not angels or rulers,
not things present, not things to come . . .
can separate us from the love of God.

—ROMANS 8:38-39

Wake up.
Live passionately.
Step outside your comfort zone.
Choose the height, breadth, the depth of *life*,
even while honoring the subtle and the tender.

Listen to others.
Ask.
Listen again.
Leave yourself behind.
When you return to your own concerns,
you will be enriched.

Imagine: and imagine *thrillingly*.
Let your ideals be worthy of your time and gaze.
Offer God, your loved ones, your friends,
all those passing strangers,
and particularly yourself,
every bit of who you are becoming.

Risk. Taste. Reach out. Reach inward.
Speak up for what moves your heart.
Sing. Dance. Play. Laugh and cry.
Praise extravagantly.
Be wrong, often.
Worry much less about being "right."
Live with love blazing from your eyes.

Don't hover over what is petty.
Wipe small-minded thinking from your mind.
Don't placate, don't shrink, don't shirk, don't hide.
Stretch out your arms.
Open your chest.
Caress the earth with the soles of your feet.

Breathe.
Forgive. And again, forgive.
Close your eyes. Then open them once more.
Breathe.
Breathe into this precious moment.
It will not come again.
You will not come again.
Treasure this life, this moment,
this love, this everything.
Every thing.
Thanks be, oh thanks be to God.

—S.D.

Only you, you alone, *are*.
We, however, wander forth until finally
our passing is so immense
that you arise: a moment
more beautiful and sudden
arising in love, or enchanted
in the contradictions of work.

I am yours, yours, regardless of time's
passage. I am commanded from you, and
to you. In the meantime,
the garland hangs by chance—unless you
take it up, up, up. And
look: festival!

—*Rainer Maria Rilke*
(*Translated by Mark S. Burrows*)

No need to leave your home in search of flowers.
Oh dear friend, save yourself that journey.

Inside your own self flowers bloom!
Each flower has a thousand petals
where you can rest.

Resting, you will glimpse beauty
within the body, and beyond it.
Before gardens. After gardens.

. . . Inside Love is more joy than you could begin to know.
Even when the sky is cloudless, rain pours down.
There are entire rivers of light.
The universe is charged with a single kind of love.

—*Kabir*

No need to run after the past.
Oh, and no need either to race toward the future.
The past is over.
The future is yet to come!

By looking deeply at things as they are now,
now, in this very moment,
the seeker becomes both calm and free.

Discover this for yourself today.
Waiting for tomorrow to find this out is too late.
Death can come at any time.

When you know how to live mindfully,
seeing things as they are today,
you will also know what it means to govern your own mind.
You will know what it means to be free.
You will truly have a perfect day.

—*Adapted from the Bhaddekaratta Sutta*

Seek—until you find.

—*Gospel of Thomas 2*

We are responsible for our own wrong-doing.
We are responsible for our own right-doing.
We are responsible for our own purity.
We are responsible for our own
ignorance. And wisdom.
No one can enlighten another.

Don't neglect your own moral development,
distracted by others' needs.
Learn first,
before teaching others.
Let each of you find the truth.
Then devote yourself to
fulfilling it.

—*The Dhammapada 12:9–10*

Avoid doing harm.
Do good.
Purify your heart. *[See clearly.]*
That is the teaching of the buddhas.

—*The Dhammapada 14:5*

Prayers for
Our World

How moving it is to discover that you can pray for all those who share our world, as well as for yourself and the people you know best. Experiencing that prayerful connection, your inner and outer worlds grow larger—and far more secure. They also grow more truthful. Our interdependence is absolute. Whatever our cultural or religious affiliations, we are members of a single human and divine family. The universality of the prayers throughout this book emphasizes this and reflects it.

The ocean has just a single taste,
and that is the taste of salt.
The true way is just a single way,
and that is the way of freedom.

Whether you are expressing your prayers through your acts of kindness to others, through study and growing insights, through community engagement, or through shared or individual prayer, you become part of the healing that the world so urgently needs.

Contemporary Zen teacher Thich Nhat Hanh has been an inspirational guide in my own life. He writes, "When the energies of compassion, understanding, and mindfulness are present, wisdom is more likely to arise. We do not change ourselves alone, but we change the collective consciousness. That collective consciousness [or 'one mind'] is the key to all change."

Prayer supports us to grow in wisdom and love. Praying for our world and all who share it, we affirm our essential unity with all of existence—and we understand it with increasing confidence and depth. The "other" becomes our neighbor. Our neighbor becomes central in our concerns. This is prayer at its most transformative. It is the most powerful antidote possible to individualism and to isolation. *And you can experience this.*

Prayer can teach you to protect and heal the physical world on which we depend. Even more tenderly and profoundly, prayer can teach you to care inclusively for humanity and the world's creatures. And to do so regardless of whether people are "like you" or share your views. What's more, prayer's good news doesn't end there.

As you pray for the well-being of all, you will find yourself also embracing parts of your own self or of your own past that you may have been tempted to abandon or exile. Realizing through prayer that all of life is sacred, and that *your entire life is sacred*, those shames and sorrows may loom far less dramatically. In fact, as your inner story changes, they may simply become part of a much bigger and more generous picture of who you are and how you are living.

"With my thoughts I circle with the world" is testament to the visionary power of the human imagination and also to the power of prayer. The more freely we circle our world with love, the freer we also become to embrace our own unique, whole and holy existence. Blessed be.

Send Thy peace O Lord, which is perfect and everlasting,
that our souls may radiate peace.
Send Thy peace, O Lord,
that we may think, act and speak harmoniously.
Send Thy peace O Lord,
that we may be contented and thankful for Thy bountiful gifts.
Send Thy peace O Lord,
that amidst our worldly strife we may enjoy Thy bliss.
Send Thy peace O Lord,
that we may endure all, tolerate all, in the thought of
Thy grace and mercy.
Send Thy peace O Lord,
that our lives may become a Divine vision and, in Thy light,
all darkness may vanish.
Send Thy peace O Lord, our Father and Mother,
that we Thy children on Earth may all
unite in a single family.

—*Hazrat Inayat Khan*

May all beings
be filled with happiness and peace.

May all beings everywhere, the strong and the weak,
the tall and short,
the powerful and the forgotten, those who are wise
and those who are not wise,
be filled with happiness and peace.

May all beings everywhere, seen and unseen,
those who live near me and those who live far from me,

those who are already born and those who are yet to be born,
be filled with happiness and peace.

Let no one deceive another person.
Let no one despise or disrespect another person.
Let no one wish in anger that someone else would suffer.

Just as a mother protects her child with her life,
and saves her only child from harm,
so we can let that unconditional love grow for all beings.

Let our love flow outward through the entire universe.
Let it flow to its height, depth and breadth.
This love is unconditional.

Then, as we stand or walk, as we sit or lie down,
as long as we are alert and remember,
we can strive for this with a single mind.
Our lives can bring heaven to earth.

—*Adapted from the Sutta Nipata*

The ocean has just a single taste,
and that is the taste of salt.
The true way is just a single way,
and that is the way of freedom.

—*From the Majjhima Nikaya*

May we recognize our unity!
May our voices rise in harmony!
May our minds turn in a single direction!
May our prayers bring us together!
May our resolution be unshakeable!
Let us be honest with our feelings.
Let us be united in our hearts.
Let us be one in our highest intentions.
Let the perfection of our interdependence,
be clear to us.

—From the Rig Veda

To attain the Truth underlying all religions,
go beyond religion.

—Meher Baba

You are the Great God of all the Earth and the Heavens.
We are so insignificant.
In us there are many defects,
But the power is yours to make
and to do what we cannot do.
You know all about us.
For coming down to earth you were despised and mocked and bru-
tally treated
because of those same defects in the men of those days.
And for those men you prayed because they did not understand
what they were doing, and that you came only for what is right.
O Lord, help us who roam about.

Help us who have been placed in Africa and
have no dwelling place of our own.
Give us back a dwelling place.
O God, all power is yours in Heaven and Earth.
Amen.

—*Chief Hosea Kutako*

In the fullness of time bring us,
with every tribe and language and people and nation,
to feast at the banquet
prepared from the foundation of the world.

—*Eucharist prayer*

When people have evolved . . . they begin to use a still
higher form of prayer.
That prayer is the adoration of the immanence of
God in the sublimity of nature . . .
It is a prayer, not to a God in heaven,
but to a God living both in heaven and on earth.

—*Hazrat Inayat Khan*

It is no longer appropriate to think
only in terms of *my* nation or country, let alone my village.

If we are to overcome the problems we face,
we need a sense of universal responsibility rooted in love
and kindness for our human brothers and sisters . . .

The very survival of humankind depends upon people
developing a concern for the whole of humanity.

—*His Holiness the 14th Dalai Lama*

The universe comes into being through
the Mother of the world.
By knowing the Mother,
we come to know her children.
By coming to know her children,
we come to know Her.

So united are they,
one does not exist
without the other.

—*Tao Te Ching, Vs. 52*

The natural world is the mental world
made visible.
The seen is the mirror of the unseen . . .
The material and the mental are not two detached
arcs in the universe,
they are two halves of a complete circle.

—*James Allen*

May the world be at peace.
May those with restless minds become serene.
May all learn to think about and care for others.
May their minds be engaged with what is uplifting.
And may our hearts be filled with selfless love for the Lord.

—*Bhagavata Purana 5.18.9*

To study the way of the Buddha is to study oneself.
To study oneself is to forget oneself.
To forget oneself is to be enlightened by everything in this world.
To be enlightened by everything,
is to surrender one's body and mind.

—*Teaching attributed to the Buddha*

What is peace?
Peace is a continuous act of creation.
Realizing that life is precious in all its forms,
we come to see an essential truth.
We are guardians of one another—and of the earth.

Recognizing our power to heal,
we find compassion.
With compassion, comes trust.
With trust, comes openness.
With openness, comes connection.
With connection, comes understanding.
With understanding, comes peace.

Peace is not an absence of conflict.
Peace is a willingness to deal with conflict intelligently.

Taste peace in your own mouth.
Feel the touch of peace on your own skin.
Let your ears fill with the sounds of peace.
Feel the longings for peace that fill your own heart.
Let your mind rest on the word peace.
Open to what peace can bring to you and others.

Without taking a single step from this place,
your thoughts can encircle the world.

—S.D.

Radiant is the World Soul,
Full of splendor and beauty.

The pure righteous do not complain of the dark,
but increase the light.
They do not complain of evil,
but increase justice.
They do not complain of heresy,
but increase faith.
They do not complain of ignorance,
but increase wisdom.

—RABBI ABRAHAM ISAAC KOOK

I am the divine seed within all beings.
Nothing and no one could exist without me.
Whatever in this world is fine,
whatever radiates intelligence or beauty,
know that it pulses with
my unlimited radiance.
With a mere fragment of myself,
I permeate and support the entire universe.

—Bhagavad Gita 10:39, 41–42

My prayer today is to allow nature to teach me,
to teach all of us,
to allow nature to heal me,
to heal all of us,
and for this to happen while we pause long enough to ask, "What's needed?"
And then to do what's needed.
And to see those choices as acts of love.
Acting with greater love toward the world,
it will be impossible for us not to act with greater love toward ourselves.
Our spiritual health—our plain joy in living, as well as our survival—
depends on consciousness and love.
It helps so much to remember that we cannot control the physical world.
We are part of the physical world.
It lives in us; we live in it.
What we can control is how we behave within our physical
universe and toward it.
We can change our thinking from fear or even despair for the earth and for
ourselves to appreciation and unlimited compassion.
Let us pray.

Let life flow.
May we touch the earth lightly.
May we cultivate beauty and nourishment wherever we can.
May we drink and use water carefully and gratefully.
May we plant thoughtfully, tend, harvest and give thanks.
May we swim with wonder.
May we regard the stars with awe.
May we bathe in the light of the moon.
May we be warmed by the sun.
May we protect ourselves from what is harsh.
May we stay open to what is tender and healing.
May we touch and be touched by the life force that we share.
And, most humbly, may we know Spirit in it all.

May we live in peace.
Blessed be.

—*S.D.*

Every war, every conflict
between human beings
has come about because
of some argument
about how things are described.

This craziness is totally unnecessary!
Just beyond the words that push us apart
a table waits.
Hospitality. Companionship.
They wait for us to make ourselves comfortable.

What we praise is one!
It makes sense that the praise is also one!

So many jugs are emptied into an infinite basin.
So many religions.
So much singing.
Just one song!

The differences are merely illusion. Or maybe pride.
Sunlight itself looks slightly different
on this wall rather than on that.
It may look quite different again
on a third.
Yet, it's just one light!

These clothes, these personalities: all borrowed
from that same light.

When we praise with a full heart,
we return light to Light.

—*Rumi*

God created man and woman in his own likeness.
In the image of God he created them.
Man and woman he created them.
And God blessed them.

And God saw everything that he had made.
And behold, it was very good.

—*Genesis 1:27–28, 31*

Blessed is the One who has compassion on the earth.
Blessed is the One who has compassion for all creatures.

—*The Baruch She'amar morning prayer*

Life's most persistent and urgent question is,
"What are you doing for others?"

—*Martin Luther King Jr.*

In quiet reflection:
Check the atmosphere that you create
with your thinking.
Before any word is spoken,
you announce your state of mind.

Check the atmosphere that you create
through how you value yourself.
When you speak to and of others,
you announce your state of mind.

Check the atmosphere that you create.
It is in your power to
lift the spirits of others,
to lift the spirits of your own self.

See for yourself that when you meet life
from your divine center,
it restores and reflects your treasured
peace of mind.

—*S.D.*

May there be peace on earth,
May there be peace in the atmosphere and
in the heavens.
May the waters be peaceful.
And also the plants.
May the Lord bring us peace.
May sincere prayers and invocations for peace
generate harmony and happiness everywhere.
Through these reflections that resolve and dissolve
violence and conflicts
we make peaceful anything on earth that would
disrupt our peace.

Let the earth become wholly rich in its blessings.
Let everything in it and on it be bountiful for us.

—From *Atharva Veda 19*

I am aware of the Divine within me.
Peace, quiet and confidence flow through my thought.

I see through all confusion to the one Divine Presence
at the center of everything.

—*Ernest Holmes*

Don't fear the changes that are coming in your life.
Instead, look forward to them with hope.
God, whose very own you are,
will lead you safely through all things.
And when it's more than you can bear,
God will bear you in His arms.

Don't fear, either, what may happen tomorrow.
The same understanding Father
who cares for you today,
will care for you tomorrow, and every day.

He will shield you from suffering.
Or He will give you the depth of strength to bear it.
Be at peace.
Put aside all anxieties. Calm your thinking.
Be at peace.

—*Adapted from a prayer attributed to Francis de Sales*

May this land be blessed by the Lord,
with precious gifts from heaven above,
and from the deep that lies beneath:
with the choicest fruits of the sun,
with the rich yield of harvests;
with the greatness of ancient mountains;
with the abundance of everlasting hills;
with treasures of the earth,
in its marvellous perfection.

—*Deuteronomy 33:13–16*

My theology is complete,
if you but grant me an omnipotent and just Creator
I need nothing more.
All the tempests in the various religious teapots
around me do seem so far off,
so young, so green, so petty!
I know I was there once,
it must have been ages ago,
and it seems impossible.
"God is love," comprises my whole system of ethics . . .

—*HANNAH TATUM WHITALL SMITH*

Let your generosity be spacious,
free of conditions and of limits.

Do good!
Do good not for your own sake only
but for the sake of everyone in the universe.

. . . Those who become truly wise see
that the infinite variety of forms in this world are not
a distraction or hindrance to spiritual understanding:
they are a healing medicine in themselves.
How is this so?

It's because they are seen and perceived as interdependent.
They have no separate self.
They express not just the mystery but also the energy
of a wholly-encompassing love.

Not only the truly wise but each one of us is living
in a world of infinite connections.
We dwell in an unbounded infinity of love.

—*From the Prajnaparamita*

When anger, fear, resentment,
hatred, jealousy or bitterness exist
in our community,
even at the level of thought,
there cannot be peace.

Peace begins with me.
When I take responsibility
for changing my consciousness,
another giant step
toward world peace
is taken.

—*Judith Pemell*

Calling In of the Four Directions

We come from the East—the North—the West—the South.
We come from diverse backgrounds, cultures and faith traditions,
delighting in difference and sharing a commitment to our
vision of life as a shared sacred journey.

Let us orient ourselves in this place to the many
dimensions of Being and Becoming:

(Turning first to the East)

Air in the East: Inspire us with clarity, help us discern how best to engage our spiritual purpose, bless our endeavors to grow in wisdom and courage.

Silence

(Turning to the North)

Fire in the North: Kindle the fire in our hearts so that our warmth, generosity and kindness may shine forth with new vigour; illuminate the pathways of spirit for us, help our spiritual enthusiasm burn brightly.

Silence

(Turning to the West)

Water in the West: Let the constant power of your ocean currents flow in us; may your life-giving rain water our seeds of spiritual intention.
Connect us to the wellspring of the Universal Heart, to the religion of loving kindness to which we all belong.

Silence

(Turning to the South)

Earth in the South: Strengthen our bodies and our souls as we come together in hope, tend us as we meet with open hearts, anchor us so that we can ground our compassion and commitment in our beautiful land.

Silence

(Facing into the Centre)

And the Centre: Greetings, Spirit of this place! Greetings, ancestors! Greetings to all beings! And, most essentially, let us acknowledge we open to Spirit, to the great Mystery expressing as the One and the Many, as we come to learn, worship and share a sacred and accepting fellowship together.

—Helen Palmer

Holy One,
I see wonder everywhere.
I also see change,
chaos, darkness.
And then light again.
I see night falling,
dawn rising,
gray skies giving way to blue, to black
and then to blue again.
I see buds, blossoms, bare branches.
Sun rising. Sun setting.
I see variety so subtle that I cannot register it
and so extreme that I am in awe of it.
Keep my inner eye clear.
Let me *see* truly.
Let me see your beauty also in
what is fading, fragile, easily forgotten.
Let me wonder, often.
Let me pause, often.
Let me notice, often.
Let me take nothing for granted.
Let me accept change gracefully.

Let my horizons continue to expand.
Let me see the subtle and the small.

Blessed be.

—*S.D.*

Breath is the clue to the interdependence of one's being with earth
and with Spirit,
for the breath draws your consciousness into the Breath of All
Breath, into the Source,
into the awareness of the
Divine Breath breathing through you.

The breath also links you to this earth because as you breathe out,
the earth and its plant forms breathe in.

They breathe out what you breathe in.

Let this interdependence inspire in you a desire to look
for the unity in life,
a desire to cherish nature as a source of life—
and also as an expression of the Source Itself.

Everything is an expression of the Divine Spirit:
on the earth, in the skies
and in the seas.

Visible and invisible,
it is all the manifestation of the One Divine Breath breathing
through you.

Visible and invisible,
it is all manifestation of the One.

—*A TEACHING FROM HEARTCENTRE*

I regard all beings equally.
Everyone is precious to me.
But those who are devoted:
they know me to be in them.
As they are in me.

—*Bhagavad Gita 9:29*

There are many roads,
but only one Path.
The prodigal soul must return to its Father,
and start the homeward journey.
This is essentially a journey through self
toward the real Self,
toward God,
and union with Him.

—*Adi K. Irani*

The silence of a temple.
The cicada's cry
enters the rocks.

— *Basho Matsuo*

From the nose
of that giant Buddha
a swallow flies out.

—*Kobayashi Issa*

Come let us go up to the mountain of the Lord,
to the house of the God of Jacob,
that he may teach us his ways,
and that we may choose his path . . .

. . . And we shall beat our swords into ploughshares,
and our spears into pruning hooks.
Nation shall not lift up sword against nation.
And neither shall they learn war any more.

—*Isaiah 2:3, 4*

I celebrate myself, and sing myself,
And what I assume you shall assume,
For every atom belonging to me as good belongs to you.
I loaf and invite my soul,
I lean and loaf at my ease observing a spear of summer grass . . .

I am larger, better than I thought.
I did not know I held so much goodness.

All seems beautiful to me,
I can repeat over to men and women,
You have done such good to me,
I would do the
same to you . . .

. . . Now I see the secret of the making of the best persons,
It is to grow in the open air, and to eat and sleep with the earth.

—*Walt Whitman*

Extracts from "Song of Myself" and

"Song of the Open Road"

Each of us comes from the Unnameable One [*Ein Sof*].
We are all included in it.
Our expression of it is what lets us live!
It sustains all existence.
We eat vegetables.
Some of us eat animals.
Yet we are nourished by something beyond this.

Though life extends infinitely,
each thing is joined within it.
One. The same.
All included. All abiding.

Investigate this!
Sparks of insight will come and go.
You may discover a secret here. Or there.
You may even discover the mystery of God
on your own.

—MOSES BEN JACOB CORDOVERO

You are in the universe
and the universe is in you.

—THICH NHAT HANH, IN THE MIRACLE OF MINDFULNESS

My wisdom comes from the Highest Source.
I greet that wisdom in you.

—MAHATMA GANDHI

The Great Goddess is Light itself and supreme.
Emanating from Her body are rays
in thousands,
two thousands,
a hundred thousand, tens of millions.
The numbers are impossible to calculate.
It is by and through Her that all things shine:
things that move and things that don't move.
It is by the light of this Devi
that all things
are brought to life.

—*From the Bhairava Yamala*

See yourself in others and others in your own self.
You will have nothing to fear.

The Lord of Love shines in every heart.
Seeing him in all, those who are wise
go beyond selfishness, and serve all.
Loving all. Serving all.
The Lord is their joy.
The Lord is their rest.
Seeing the truth of this, meditating,
and choosing wisely,
you can have this joy.
You can see the Eternal Self shining
in a pure heart.

—*Upanishadic teaching; Mundaka Upanishad 1:4–5*

When you see others as your sister or brother, you see God.

—CLEMENT OF ALEXANDRIA

Life is meant to be lived from a Center,
a divine Center.
Each one of us can live such a life of amazing power
and peace and serenity,
of integration and confidence . . . on one condition—
that is, *if we really want to.*
There is a divine Abyss within us all,
a holy Infinite Center,
a Heart, a Life
who speaks in us
and through us
to the world.

—THOMAS R. KELLY, IN A TESTAMENT OF DEVOTION

The light of unity can illuminate the whole earth.

—BAHA'U'LLAH

With what shall I come before the Lord,
and bow myself before God?
Shall I come before Him with burnt offerings or sacrifices?
Will the Lord be pleased with thousands of rams,
with ten thousand rivers of oil?
Shall I give my firstborn for my sins,
the fruit of my body to atone for the sins of my soul?

He has told you, oh humankind, what is good,
and everything that the Lord asks of you.
It is to do justice, to love kindness,
and to walk humbly in friendship with your God.

—*Micah 6:6–8*

May the sun bring you energy by day.
May the moon restore you by night.
May the rain wash away your worries.
May the breeze blow life to your being.
May you walk gently in the world.
May you see its beauty
all the days of your life.

—*Traditional Navajo blessing*

Walk and touch happiness every moment.
Each step brings a fresh breeze.
Each step makes a flower bloom under our feet.
Kiss the earth with your feet.
Print on earth your love and happiness.

—*Thich Nhat Hanh*

Christ has no body on earth. Only yours.
No hands. Only yours.
No feet. Only yours.
It's through your eyes that Christ's compassion
reaches the world.
It's with your feet that He can go about,
doing good.
It's with your hands that he can bless us all,
right now.

—*Teresa of Avila*

Must I really fret about enlightenment?
No matter what road I travel,
I am going home.

—*Shinso*

A tree so great it needs both arms to circle its trunk
grew from a tiny seedling.

A towering pagoda
was built by placing one brick upon another.

A journey of a thousand miles
begins with a single step.

—*Lao-Tzu*

For all that's been,
for all that now is,
for all there is to come,
we give thanks.

May we live as a source of
happiness and peace
for others,
and for ourselves.

May we live lovingly.
May we live appreciatively.
May our own lives bring heaven to earth.
Blessed be.

—*S.D.*

Index of Names and Principal Texts

Acknowledgments

For original prayers or translations of prayers that have not previously been published, I would like to thank for their gracious permission the following individuals: Georgia Carr and Susan MacFarlane from Heartcentre (www.heartcentre.com.au); Dr. Kim Cunio, Reverend Helen Palmer, Judith Pemell and Reverend Hilary Star. I owe particular thanks to the immensely gifted and generous poet and scholar Dr. Mark S. Burrows (www.msburrows.com) for use of his exquisite recent translations of two poems by Rainer Maria Rilke and of the complete "Ravensburg Prayer." Thank you, too, to my dear friend writer Hanan al-Shaykh for her translation of Rabi'a's words from the original Arabic, which appeared in a slightly different version also in my book *Seeking the Sacred*. Copyright in these prayers and translations remains with their authors.

I would also like to thank the following copyright holders for their gracious permission to publish: Sufi Order International for prayers by Hazrat Inayat Khan; the UK Retreat Association and Mary Holiday for "God of stillness and creative action"; B. K. Sister Jayanti for lines originally published in *God's Healing Power: How Meditation Can Help Transform Your Life,* published by Sterling Publishing, New York, © BKIS Publications, London, available at www.bkpublications.com;

Paraclete Press, Orleans, Massachusetts, and Mark S. Burrows for "With a branch that was never like that one," Prayer [34], in *Prayers of a Young Poet: Rainer Maria Rilke*, translated and introduced by Mark S. Burrows, © 2013 by Mark S. Burrows, www.paracletepress.com; Hay House UK and Andrew Harvey for lines originally published in *The Hope: A Guide to Sacred Activism,* © 2009 by Andrew Harvey, published by Hay House, available at www.hayhouse.com; Heartways Press, Greenfield, Massachusetts, and Paul Ferrini for his lines from *Grace Unfolding,* www.paulferrini.com; Allen & Unwin Pty Ltd and this author for lines from *The Universal Heart: A Practical Guide to Love,* © 2000 by Wise Angels Pty Ltd, www.stephaniedowrick.com.

With a very happy heart, I wish to thank Dr. Jane Goodall for her invaluably insightful reading of an earlier draft of this book and the depth and constancy of her literary encouragement. I want to thank Judith Ackroyd and Hilary Star for their magnificent friendship, and Jane Moore for exceptional care, laughter and loyalty, for shared prayers, and, once again, for her deep knowledge and practice of Sufi philosophy and teachings. During the time of writing this book I have also continued to work with several wonderful souls whose support and collaboration I cherish and wish particularly to acknowledge: musician and composer Dr. Kim Cunio; travel companion and workshop organizer William Suganda; my cohost on the Universal Heart Book Club online project, Walter Mason; and meditation teacher and academic Dr. Kalvinder Shields, who has become a "prayer companion" in ways that are an unfolding blessing.

I would also like to thank my beloved daughter, Kezia Tieck, and her darling daughter, Madeleine, for unfailing love and inspiration that fills my life with joy. I would like to thank my son, Gabriel Dowrick, for his treasured presence in my life and for his consistent good humor. My work at Mana Retreat Center, Coromandel, New

Zealand, and as interfaith minister at Pitt Street Uniting Church, Sydney, has significantly supported the development of my prayer and teaching life. I would like to thank each person who attends the retreats and services that allow us to grow together, and, very particularly, Reverend Ian Pearson, formerly minister at Pitt Street Uniting Church and a great friend to our interfaith community there, as well as Donna Idol, who has shared and supported Mana retreats both as Mana's manager and as a committed and inspiring participant.

My writing life is enhanced in crucial ways by gifted publishers who continue to offer an exceptional depth and constancy of interest. I am particularly grateful with this book to my Tarcher/Penguin publisher, Joel Fotinos, for it was he who stood with me in front of the bookshelves in his New York office and let me believe this book might be possible. It has been so lovely to write, so instructive, calming and consoling, and I have Joel to thank for that. Publishers are almost always talented; far better than that, Joel demonstrates a rare largeness of heart and vision and I consider myself extremely blessed to be among "his" writers. Also at Tarcher I wish to thank Andrew Yackira for much patience and best editorial care, as well as copy editor Jane Ludlam, and designer Amanda Dewey. Publishing is increasingly a cooperative experience. My gratitude to my Australian publishers is unlimited, especially to Sue Hines, Allen & Unwin's Publishing Director, for the unwavering commitment she has to my work and her deep understanding of my best intentions for it; to senior editor Christa Munns, cover designer Lisa White and my superb publicist Louise Cornegé: their combined gifts are all that I could wish for and this book celebrates that. I don't want to forget, either, all the behind-the-scenes people at both publishing houses, particularly those who work in sales and marketing. Readers as well as writers depend on their efforts, just as they also depend on a shrinking band of committed, determined booksellers. I want to say thank you so much to each and every one of them for everything they will do to pass these words, these prayers, these sacred good wishes to everyone who may seek or need them.

May all be well and happy. May all live in peace.

If you enjoyed this book, visit

www.tarcherbooks.com

and sign up for Tarcher's e-newsletter to receive
special offers, giveaway promotions, and
information on hot upcoming releases.

**TARCHER
PENGUIN**

Great Lives Begin with Great Ideas

Connect with the Tarcher Community

• • •

Stay in touch with favorite authors
Enter weekly contests
Read exclusive excerpts!
Voice your opinions!

Follow us

 Tarcher Books

 @TarcherBooks

If you would like to place a bulk order
of this book, call 1-800-847-5515.

In the Company of Rilke • (ISBN: 9781585428670)
Drawing on her deep understanding of Rilke's unique gifts to readers, as well as her own personal spiritual seeking and literary journey, Dr. Stephanie Dowrick offers an intimate appreciation of this most exceptional poet and his transcendent work, as well as a rare grasp of the spiritual yearnings his work expresses. The book includes more than one hundred of Rilke's most exquisite poems.

Everyday Kindness • (ISBN: 9780399160899)
In this immediately encouraging book, Dr. Stephanie Dowrick takes kindness as her inspiration and theme. Through practical topics as varied as parenting, power, moods (and food), self-confidence, identity and work, she shows how everyday kindness can smooth our lives, saving us from much unnecessary stress and tension, and securing for us new levels of confidence, appreciation and trust.